Cin

ders

(Feu la cendre)

J

by Jacques Derrida

D

University of Nebraska Press   Lincoln & London

Trans*lated, edited, and with an introduction*

by

Ned Lukacher

Library of Congress Cataloging in Publication Data

Derrida, Jacques.

[Feu la cendre. English]

Cinders / by Jacques Derrida ; translated, edited, and with an introduction by Ned Lukacher.

p. cm.

Translation of: Feu la cendre.

Includes bibliographical references.

ISBN 0-8032-1689-0 (alk. paper)

1. Play on words. 2. Homonyms. 3. Ambiguity

I. Lukacher, Ned, 1950- II. Title.

P304.D4713 1991

90-27742

401'.41-dc20 CIP

contents

Introduction

Mourning

Becomes

Telepathy

Ned Lukacher

I shall show the cinders of my spirits
Through the ashes of my chance

SHAKESPEARE, Antony and Cleopatra

Why does Jacques Derrida speak of the trace in terms of ash and cinder (*cendre*)? "I would prefer *ashes*," Derrida has said, "as the better paradigm for what I call the trace — something that erases itself totally, radically, while presenting itself."[1] In *Cinders,* Derrida writes that cinders are "the best paradigm for the trace," better than "the trail," "the fraying," "the furrow," or the many other names he has given to the trace structure since his first publications from the 1960s. But he has also written that cinder is only one name among others for "these remains without remainder": "Trace or cinder. These names are as good as any other."[2] Cinder is at once the best name for the absence of a truly proper name for that which holds all beings and entities in presence, and by the same token just another name that cannot begin to assess its distance or proximity to the final proper name (or names) of the truth of Being, whose very existence remains undecidable. Cinder is the best name, in Derrida's estimation, among all the names that have thus far presented themselves, but it is merely another name when considered in relation to the still withheld truth of Being. The naming of a cinder thus resists presenting itself as the privileged name or metaphor for that which brings things to presence and sustains them there. It is at the same time a name that resists the temptation to make the play of metaphor itself synonymous with the truth of Being. Cinders are neither proper nor metaphorical names; cinders name another relation, not to the truth as such, but to its possibility.

Why are there cinders rather than nothing? Why does language bear something within itself that somehow signals a language beyond language, that signals *that* there are conditions for the possibility of a language without saying *what* those conditions are? Why does language bear within itself the traces of something that cannot be exhausted by pragmatics and historicity, something from which the *pragmata* of history themselves arise? "Cinders there are" (*Il y a là cendre*), "there are cinders there," "there" where the marks of a divisible materiality within language, within its syntactic and linguistic stuff, trace the infinitesimal cinder quarks that remain from whatever it is that makes it possible and necessary that a language comes into being. Cinders are the quarks of language, neither proper names nor metaphors, the traces of neither ontotheology nor of the generalization of metaphor, naming neither truth nor its impossibility, but all the while keeping a space open into which the truth, or its impossibility, might come, a space, as Derrida calls it, for the in-vention, the *in-venire,* the in-coming of the other.[3]

Cinders are all that remain of the path that might someday lead back (or forward) to the origin of language, the path that opens the possibilities of the metaphoric and the literal without being reducible to either of them. Though it is one name among others for this path, trace, or trait that separates and joins the figurality of poetic or metaphoric naming to the philosophic thinking of the literal, a cinder is nevertheless a very specific name whose associations with heat, fire, and

---

1. Jacques Derrida, "On Reading Heidegger: An Outline of Remarks to the Essex Colloquium," *Research in Phenomenology* 17 (1987): 177.

2. Jacques Derrida, *Schibboleth: Pour Paul Celan* (Paris: Galilée, 1986), 73. My translation.

3. "But one does not make the other come, one lets it come by preparing for its coming. The coming of the other or its coming back is the only possible arrival, but it is not invented, even if the most genial inventiveness is needed to prepare to welcome it" (Jacques Derrida, "Psyche: Inventions of the Other," trans. Catherine Porter, in *Reading De Man Reading,* ed. Lindsay Waters and Wlad Godzich [Minneapolis: University of Minnesota Press, 1989], 60).

conflagration figure prominently in Derrida's usage. In the warmth of a cinder one can feel the effects of the fire even if the fire itself remains inaccessible, outside cognition though not without leaving a trace. Thinking and poetic naming lead us only so far on a cinder path, for cinders cool and fall to ash and the path leads no further. Does something within language really burn? Does language bear within itself the remains of a burning? *Cinders* is about the fire that is still burning at the origin of language, the not yet literal but more than figurative fire that can be felt in the cinders of a language.

The fire has always already consumed access to the origin of language and thus to the truth of being. But by leaving cinder remains, it allows the relation between the coming of language and the truth of being to persist, to smolder within the ashes. Cinders name both the extreme fragility and the uncanny tenacity of this relation.

A cinder is a very fragile entity that falls to dust, that crumbles and disperses. But cinders also name the resilience and the intractability of what is most delicate and most vulnerable. *Il y a là cendre* literally means "it has ashes there, there." By rendering the idiomatic *il y a* by "there is," we install the intransitive verb "to be" where, properly speaking, it does not belong, for in the French idiom what is in question is not the "being" of the entity but its "there-ness." As in the German *Es gibt* (literally, "it gives"; idiomatically, "there is"), *il y a* makes no determination concerning the ontology of the essent. Each time we read the refrain *il y a là cendre,* "cinders there are," we should remember that the delicate vulnerability of a cinder leaves open the question of its being or non-being. We should hear within "cinders there are" something like "it has cinders," or "it gives cinders," or "cinders persist," where what "it" may be and what "persistence" might entail are among the questions the phrase poses without implying that it already has the answers.

Martin Heidegger also emphasizes the delicate nature of the relation between language and truth; between figure and idea; between the thick condensations of *Dichten,* or poetic naming, and the quasi-conceptual determinations of thinking, or *Denken,* which are, he writes, "held apart by a delicate yet luminous difference" (*zarte aber helle Differenz*).[4] Though this delicately glowing "rift" (*Riss*) holds metaphor and the literal apart, this holding is itself a relation (*Bezug*) that keeps them from being "separated in a relationless void" (*ins Bezuglose abgeschieden*). In *Cinders* this luminous glow emanates from within the ashes, and now it is less a question of seeing the light than of feeling the heat. It is the event in which this luminous rift "incises" itself into *Dichten* and *Denken* and thus draws them, engraves them, sets them into "the design [*Aufriss*] of their neighboring nature" that Heidegger names the *Ereignis,* which for Heidegger always entails a double movement in which language is incised by the withdrawal of the unnameable otherness of its origin and is thereby set into its own proper nature. As Derrida remarks in his reading of this passage of Heidegger's "The Nature of Language," the incisive movement of *Ereignis* "is structurally in withdrawal": "Its inscription [. . .] *occurs only by effacing itself.*"[5] In *Cinders* the appropriative-disappropriative structure of *Ereignis* is enacted through the withdrawal of the fire that continues to burn in a cinder. The coming of language as a means of thought and expression is always also the withdrawal within language of the trace, the trait, the *re-trait* of its concealed origin. Heidegger writes elsewhere that "language is the most delicate [*zarteste*] and thus the most vulnerable [*anfälligste*] vibration holding everything within the suspended

4. Martin Heidegger, *On the Way to Language,* trans. Peter Hertz (New York: Harper & Row, 1971), 90; Martin Heidegger, *Unterwegs zur Sprache* (Pfullingen: Günther Neske, 1982), 196.

5. Jacques Derrida, "The *Retrait* of Metaphor," *Enclitic* 2 (1978): 29 (translation modified); Jacques Derrida, "Le retrait de la métaphore," in *Psyche: Inventions de l'autre* (Paris: Galilée, 1987), 88–89.

structure of the *Ereignis*" (*alles verhaltende Schwingung im schwebenden Bau des Ereignisses*).[6] It is the heat within the resonance of this oscillation that Derrida names *là cendre*. Cinder names the tender susceptibility of that vibration, that ringing, that burning within language. To hear, to speak, to write, is to feel the heat, to feel the retreat of the fire as a cinder falls, yet again, to ash.

At what temperature do words burst into flame? Is language itself what remains of a burning? Is language the effect of an inner vibration, an effect of light and heat upon certain kinds of matter? *Glas* begins and ends with an allusion to Hegel's notion of *Klang,* the "ringing" at the origin of language that Hegel discerns in the legend of the "colossal sounding statue" (*Klangstatue*) of the Memnons in ancient Thebes, which emitted a sound when struck by sunlight at sunrise.[7] It is on the border between speech and *Klang* that the path to the origin of language becomes impassable; and it is there that a cinder burns. Sound is first the escape of heat; so also for Derrida is language. *Il y a là cendre* initially presents itself to Derrida as a ringing tonality before it becomes a meaningful utterance. The ideal materiality of its broken music precedes the unfolding of its poetic and philosophic resonance. *Klang,* writes Hegel, is "the ideality of materiality" that characterizes "the transition of material spatiality into material temporality."[8] For Hegel *Klang* names the initial ringing at the beginning of time, the sound of the first burning, the sound of the fire as it rushes from absolute space into the relative space of universal creation. "The bell," writes Heidegger, thinking of Hölderlin, but perhaps also of Hegel, "– rather its *Klang* – is the song of poets. It calls into the turning of time."[9] Poets enable us to hear the tones and echoes which this *Klang* has traced into a language, whereas thinkers speak of the causes and the consequences of these traces. As Derrida's *ars metaphysica, Cinders* leads us into those spaces within the French language where one can still hear something burning, still hear the ringing in language of a burning more ancient than time and space.

Cinders bear the traces of this most ancient materiality within the empirical, extended materiality of measurable space and time. The smoldering ashes of another materiality ring from within the tonalities of a material language; within the idioms of a language burn the remains of something other than a singular idiom, the cinders of a still lost and unreadable genealogy.

"Spirit is flame," writes Heidegger, "It glows and shines."[10] Heidegger's essay "Language in the Poem: A Discussion of Georg Trakl's Poetic Work" is treated at some length in Derrida's *Of Spirit: Heidegger and the Question,* where Derrida focuses on the way Heidegger's idioms name the burning of the earliest beginning within the German language.[11] *Of Spirit* is very closely linked to the language and the problems raised in *Cinders,* for the latter text seeks within the French language the still burning traces of the most primordial beginning. In "Ghostly Twilight" (*Geistliche Dämmerung*) Trakl writes: "Forever rings [*tönt*] the sister's lunar voice / Through the ghostly night."[12] It

6. Martin Heidegger, *Identity and Difference,* trans. Joan Stambaugh (New York: Harper & Row, 1969), 38. Translation modified.

7. Jacques Derrida, *Glas,* trans. John P. Leavey, Jr., and Richard Rand (Lincoln: University of Nebraska Press, 1986), 3a, 253a.

8. G.W.F. Hegel, *Philosophy of Nature,* 3 vols., trans. M. J. Petrey (New York: Humanities Press, 1970), 2:69.

9. Martin Heidegger, *Erläuterungen zu Hölderlins Dichtung,* Bd.4 of *Gesamtausgabe,* ed. Friedrich-Wilhelm von Hermann (Frankfurt am Main: Vittorio Klostermann, 1981), 197. My translation.

10. Martin Heidegger, *On the Way to Language,* 181; "Der Geist ist Flamme. Glühend leuchtet sie" (*Unterwegs zur Sprache,* 62).

11. Jacques Derrida, *Of Spirit: Heidegger and the Question,* trans. Geoffrey Bennington and Rachel Bowlby (Chicago: University of Chicago Press, 1989), esp. 83–111.

12. Cited in Heidegger, *On the Way to Language,* 169 (*Unterwegs,* 48).

is through the ringing sound of this voice that the fire of the spirit gathers the soul of the poet. The coming of the phrase *il y a là cendre* likewise passes through this *geistliche Nacht,* this "ghostly night," where *geistliche* means, not the insufflating breath of *pneuma* or *spiritus,* but the still burning ringing of what Heidegger calls "the stiller, brighter earliness."[13]

Derrida's French in *Cinders* is scorched by the ghostly spirit that gathers and draws its idioms into relation with the secret that burns within the essence of a cinder. Georg Trakl's sister, Margarete, calls him into the "Evening Land," into the "Occident" which is the site of what the poet calls *"one* generation," *"one* kinship," *"one* flesh," *"one* gender," all of which translate "ein *Geschlecht."* Beyond the incestuous echoes that surround the enigma of Trakl's relationship with his sister, the ringing of the fire in language calls the poet to a more primordial unity. The "cinders love me," writes Derrida, "they change sex, they re-cinder themselves, they androgynocide themselves." The feminine voice of *La Cendre,* "she, the cinder," plays in *Cinders* a role not unlike that of Margarete Trakl. But, as Derrida repeatedly maintains, the gender of the cinder is highly unstable; thus, in his untranslatable French neologisms, cinders *"s'andrent,"* which rhymes with *cendre,* and they *"s'androgynocident,"* which evokes *cendre,* androgyny, and genocide. *Geist* gathers language into the cinders of "ein *Geschlecht."*

2

An open region that holds the promise of a dwelling, and provides a dwelling, is what we call a "land." The passage into the stranger's land leads through ghostly twilight.

HEIDEGGER, *"Language in the Poem"*

Toward the end of *Cinders* Derrida alludes to Friedrich Nietzsche's notion of "eternal recurrence" and to his idea that "our entire world is the cinder of innumerable *living* beings." In other words, even inanimate and inorganic matter is the cinder of what was once living. Nietzsche's idea that the universe is itself a cinder that burns and cools and then burns again anticipates Albert Einstein's notion of an expanding and perhaps contracting universe of finite mass and energy. How does finitude come to presence? How can we think of space and time as themselves figures of some nonfinite thing, figures of something "outside" a finite universe? Whence comes the light and the fire that, as Einstein remarks, "transfers mass" (*das Licht überträgt Masse*)?[14] Does the light of the fire bear an "outside" into the "inside"? Do any traces of an "outside" remain? If there are traces, are they merely unreadable remains or can we use them to reconstruct an "outside"? How can we think the difference of what lies *between* outside and inside? What is still hidden in the coming to presence of this light and in the transference of mass and energy by the fire of creation? Nietzsche's notion of the universe as cinder attempts to think the residual mass-energy of the outside that still burns on the inside.

When Derrida calls Nietzsche "something else perhaps than a thinker of the totality of entities," he is thinking of Heidegger's reading of Nietzsche as a thinker who succumbed to the metaphysician's desire to think the essence of the unhidden as something present, the desire to bring to presence the hiddenness from which all that is present emerged. Heidegger regards Nietzsche's notion of the "will to power," the essential or underlying force that determines the eternal recurrence of the finite universe over and over again, as a furious and futile imposition of the truth of beings upon the truth of Being: "The essential, historic culmination of the final metaphysical interpretation of beingness as will to power is captured in the eter-

---

13. Heidegger, *On the Way to Language,* 188 (*Unterwegs,* 71).

14. *The Swiss Years: Writings, 1900–1909,* vol.2 of *Collected Papers of Albert Einstein,* ed. John Stachel (Princeton: Princeton University Press, 1989), 268–69.

nal recurrence of the same, captured in such a way that every possibility for the essence of truth to emerge as what is most worthy of question founders."[15]

Derrida's phrase, "something else perhaps than a thinker of the totality of entities," indicates a certain departure from Heidegger's position, at least insofar as it pertains to the cinder as the trace of Nietzsche's effort to think not the essence of Being or beings but the difference between them; thus the cinder becomes the trace of a certain nonmetaphysical element in Nietzsche's thinking. The cinder thus names thinking's inability to achieve the metaphysical determination of the essence of unhiddenness.

The "*big bang,*" writes Derrida, "would have, let us say at the origin of the universe, produced a noise which we can regard as not yet having reached *us*. It is still to come and it will be up to us to capture it, to receive it."[16] This ringing noise is still an absolute nonmemory, but it may not be so elsewhere, nor may it always be this way for us, or for those after us. Here and now, we cannot think beyond the borders of our finitude.

Nietzsche describes eternal recurrence as an image in a mirror, an image of the finitude of self-reflection, and thus also of its limits. At its limits, in the place of the tain of the mirror, lies the "nothing," which "rings" the world into spatial form, between inside and outside, between a world and its concealed essence:

And do you know what "the world" is to me? Shall I show it to you in my mirror? This world: a monster of energy, without beginning, without end; a fixed, brazen quantity of energy, which becomes neither bigger nor smaller, which does not consume itself [die sich nicht verbraucht], *but only transforms itself; as a whole, of unalterable size, a household without losses and gains, but also without increases, without revenues; enclosed by "nothing" as by a boundary; not something vague or wasteful, not infinitely extended, but as a determined force enclosed in a determined space, and not a space*

that would be "empty" anywhere, but rather as force everywhere, as a play of forces and waves of force, at once one and many, increasing here and at the same time decreasing there, a sea of forces storming and raging in itself, eternally changing, eternally running back, over monstrous ages of recurrence, with an ebb and flow of its forms, out of the simplest forms striving toward the most complex, out of the stillest, most rigid, coldest forms come forth the hottest, most turbulent, most self-contradictory, and then back home again from the most abundant to the simplest, from the play of contradictions back to the pleasure of concord [Einklangs], *still affirming itself in this similarity of its courses and ages, blessing itself as that which must recur eternally, as a becoming that knows no satiety, no disgust, no weariness –: this, my* dionysian *world of eternal self-creation, of eternal self-destruction, this mystery world of twofold bliss; this, my "Beyond Good and Evil" without aim* [Ziel], *unless the joy of the circle is itself a goal, without will, unless a ring holds goodwill unto itself – would you have a* name *for this world? A solution to all its riddles? A light for you too, you most-concealed, strongest, most undaunted men of darkest midnight? –* This world is the will to power – and nothing else! *And even you yourselves are this will to power – and nothing else.*[17]

Nietzsche forgets neither the distinction between *what* the world is and *that* it is nor between the world in the mirror and what

15. Martin Heidegger, *The Will to Power as Knowledge and as Metaphysics,* vol.3 of *Nietzsche,* trans. Joan Stambaugh, David Farrell Krell, Frank A. Capuzzi (San Francisco: Harper & Row, 1987), 180–81.

16. Jacques Derrida, "Télépathie," *Furor* 2 (1981): 10. My translation.

17. Friedrich Nietzsche, *Werke,* 3 vols., ed. Karl Schlecta (Munich: Carl Hanser Verlag, 1960), 3:916–17. This is passage number 1067 in *The Will to Power.* I have consulted and modified the following two translations: *The Will to Power,* 2 vols., trans. Anthony M. Lodovici (New York: Macmillan, n.d.), 2:431–32; *The Will to Power,* trans. Walter Kaufmann and R.J. Hollingdale (New York: Random House, 1967), 549–50.

lies on the other side. The task he sets for himself, however, is to *name* this world, to name its "whatness" without mistaking it for the name of what is beyond the boundary that he calls the "nothing" (*Nichts*). The ebb and flow of the world as will to power is contained, surrounded (*umschlossen*), by a border (*Grenze*) that gives the universe the shape of a circle or a ring, a defined space in which a defined quantity of energy, heat, and light works its way through its incessant cycles of creation and annihilation. It is the voracious appetite of the world within the ring that Nietzsche calls "the will to power." The formation of the ring itself, however, is, in Nietzsche's extraordinary phrase, "without will" (*ohne Willen*), "unless a ring holds goodwill unto itself" (*wenn nicht ein Ring zu sich selber guten Willen hat*). The ring stands beyond the world as will to power, and thus bars the way to the essence of the truth of what comes to presence. In closing off our world, it opens onto something entirely other, something that goes entirely against the grain of Heidegger's characterization of Nietzsche's thinking: "As a revaluator of all values, Nietzsche testifies to the fact that he belongs ineluctably to metaphysics and thereby to its abyssal separation from *every possibility* of another commencement. Nietzsche himself does not know the distance that is measured out in this final step."[18]

The ring is the name Nietzsche gives to the possibility of this other beginning. It is his name for this last step (*dieses letzten Schrittes*), this step that traces the nonpresent within presence, the step in which one finds oneself stepping up behind oneself, going not beyond but before, not into a metaphysical cosmology but back into the enigma of the everyday. Nietzsche, *pace* Heidegger, does know the unspeakable distance that this step measures out. The ring is between the world as will to power and the still withheld essence from which a world comes to presence. It names the unreflective foil on the other side of the mirror, what Heidegger, in discussing ancient Greek philoso-phy, calls the *khorismos,* or "gap," between Being and Becoming. In Nietzsche's *Ring* we can hear the ringing of the *Klang,* the burning trace of an otherness that keeps a space open for the promise and the question of the truth of Being.

In Nietzsche's account of the ring, there is a strange economy in this passage between the *Nichts* and the *wenn nicht* that inscribes the trace of another commencement, of a nothingness that is not nothing, of an "unless," an "except when," a hesita-tion, a proviso, a "but . . . ," that opens the *between* of the *khorismos.* Nietzsche writes the trace of something beyond the world in the world, something that appears only in disappear-ing, something that disappears into the thoughtful silence of the *wenn nicht,* as if to say, "but what if, on the other side of the ring . . . ." The *Nichts* and the *wenn nicht* trace what Derrida calls a cinder, the trace here of a nonpresent "there," the re-mains of the ring between outside and inside. Heidegger says that Nietzsche's fundamental metaphysical position "can be the counterposition for our other commencement only if the latter adopts a *questioning* stance vis-à-vis the initial com-mencement – as one which in its proper originality is only now commencing." Nietzsche's putative ignorance of the "last step" serves as the pretext for the first step that is "the unfolding of a more original inquiry":

The thinker inquires into being as a whole and as such; into the world as such. Thus with his very first step he always thinks out beyond the world, and so at the same time back to it. He thinks in the direction of that sphere *within which a world becomes world. Wherever that sphere is not incessantly called by name, called aloud, wherever it is held silently in the most interior questioning, it is thought most purely and profoundly.*[19]

18. Martin Heidegger, *The Will to Power as Knowledge and as Metaphysics,* 176.

19. Martin Heidegger, *The Eternal Recurrence of the Same,* vol. 2 of *Nietzsche,* trans. David Farrell Krell (New York: Harper & Row, 1984), 206–7.

Listening for the silent trace of another origin, for the ring of the nothing, for the accord (*Einklang*) of "the most interior questioning," is precisely what Heidegger cannot discover in Nietzsche. We might call this Heidegger's *pas de Nietzsche*, Nietzsche's (non)step, Nietzsche's "no," or "no" to Nietzsche. It is in this destabilizing *pas de* . . . , in this step "out beyond the world, and so at the same time back to it," that a cinder burns.

Heidegger speaks of the trace in terms of the mystery of presence that is concealed within the privative *a* of *a-letheia*, the coming into unhiddenness, coming from beyond the ring, coming from the other side of the *khorismos* into the world.[20] The privative *a* in Heraclitus's *aletheia* or in Anaximander's *apeiron* (the un-bounded) name the nameless exception, the withdrawal that is the coming to presence of a world.

The *a* in differance likewise marks the non-negative, nameless silence that dwells within the name, the trace of something irreducible to either presence or absence within the difference between Being and beings. At the same time, Derrida's appropriation of this Heideggerian motif also disappropriates a vestigial echo in Heidegger's usage of a certain apocalyptic promise that there is a final proper name to be discovered: "This is why the thought of the letter *a* in *différance* is not the primary prescription or the prophetic annunciation of an imminent and as yet unheard-of nomination. There is nothing kerygmatic about this 'word,' provided that one perceives its decapita(liza)tion. And that one puts into question the name of the name."[21] Because we do not know whether or not there is a final proper name of Being, we will always hear a residual, silent promise of the name. What Derrida calls "an apocalyptic tone" is thus at once irresistible and menacing, a double bind. There is no way *not* to speak of "the name of the name."[22] The task of putting into question the name of the name defines Derrida's fundamental project from his earliest work to the present.

Feu la cendre, here translated as *Cinders,* was first published in 1982. The enigmatic, untranslatable phrase *il y a là cendre* first appeared in the acknowledgments to *La Dissémination* in 1972. Derrida retrospectively traces anticipatory echoes of the phrase in "Plato's Pharmacy" (1968), as well as post-1972 resonances of the phrase and the motifs it conveys in *Glas* (1974), *The Postcard* (1980), and "Telepathy" (1981), which is closely linked to the "Envois" section of *The Postcard*. Hence the shuttling back and forth from the left-hand pages, the "Animadversions," a title which means "observations" or "assessments" and is of long standing in the history of criticism (Milton and Leibniz, for example, wrote texts using this title), and which gathers together the previously published allusions to cinders and ashes from texts written between 1968 and 1980, and the right-hand pages of *Cinders,* where we find the philosophical prose poem that was written in 1982 and that is woven around the phrase "cinders there are." Which came first, the text written in 1982 or the antecedent passages that were gathered together in 1982 in response to the "newly" inscribed text of *Feu la cendre*? Which was the first step and which the last? Which is the cause and which the effect? The very construction of *Cinders* destabilizes the genealogical inquiry into antecedents and consequences in the very act of posing it. When did the gathering of cinders begin?

20. Cf. Martin Heidegger, "Plato's Doctrine of Truth," trans. John Barlow, in *Philosophy in the Twentieth Century,* ed. William Barrett and Henry D. Aiken (New York: Random House, 1962), 3:270.

21. Jacques Derrida, "Différance, " in *Margins of Philosophy,* trans. Alan Bass (Chicago: University of Chicago Press, 1982), 27.

22. Cf. Jacques Derrida, "Of an Apocalyptic Tone Recently Adopted in Philosophy," trans. John P. Leavey, Jr., *Oxford Literary Review* 6 (1984):3–37; and Jacques Derrida, "How to Avoid Speaking: Denials," trans. Ken Frieden, in *Languages of the Unsayable: The Play of Negativity in Literature and Literary Theory,* ed. Sanford Budick and Wolfgang Iser (New York: Columbia University Press, 1989), 3–70.

In order to pose the question of what constitutes a "first time" and a "last time," in order to pose the question of another beginning, Derrida listens closely to and looks closely at an unreadable phrase that appears to have been telepathically transmitted from the margins of finitude. Here the privative *a* takes the form of the silent difference between *la cendre* and *là cendre,* between "the cinder" and "there cinder." In this telecommunicated signal, "there" is precisely what oscillates; *là,* with or without the accent, is what comes in and out of tune, in and out of range; the privative *à* marks the cinder track through which this phrase has been traveling since before the beginning, the always double and divided beginning, where the nonorigin at the origin is already divided by the trace of a nonpresent "outside." *Cinders* tells of the coming of differance, of the absolutely minimal positivity of the privative *à* (with or without the accent), the instable divisibility within language that inscribes the trace of something beyond it, of its essence, inaccessible beyond the ring. The "Animadversions" (as the Latin etymology suggests, "a turning of the mind toward"), gather together the trail of ashes toward which Derrida had always somehow been turning, gather together the cinders that had always been calling to him, calling for his attention. *Cinders* is the text in which Derrida finally answers the call.

On the way to answering the call, Derrida deciphered many of the names that the master thinkers from Plato to Heidegger have given to the differance within ontological difference, sometimes without having themselves realized precisely what they were naming. These paleonymic or deconstructive readings of the names of what is most ancient, ancient and modern names for what is older than time and space, these readings turn again and again to a primordial nonpresence that is not nothing, what Derrida calls in his reading of Husserl "the irreducible nonpresence of another now."[23] *Verflechtung,* or "intertwining," is the word in Husserl's *Logical Investigations* that names

the destabilizing linkage within language between indication and expression, the irreducibility of what the sign shows prior to its appropriation by the *cogito* as an expressive means of establishing its own self-relation. Something in the sign pre-exists the ideal self-relation of the Husserlian *cogito* and in fact constitutes it rather than being constituted by it. The *Verflechtung* of indication and expression names the site of what Derrida, in his study of Husserl's *The Origin of Geometry,* called "a degradation at the interior of language."[24] The power of the sign to gather meaning and sense (*sens*) arises from this degraded nonpresence, this crumbling and fragile otherness of language that makes the sign "the worldly and exposed residence of an unthought truth"; the truth being that this something within language, which Derrida calls "writing," causes the truth "to disappear." What Derrida, still in the introduction to *The Origin of Geometry,* calls "la possibilité graphique," marks the site of a persistent instability, an uncontainable divisibility within the very essence of language that is something other than language, that is something other than sensation and cognition. The inscription (*gramma*) and the letter (*grammata*) are always already engaged to, and in the service of, the divisibility of the trace that they bear within themselves as the very condition of their coming to presence. Writing (*écriture*) is the name Derrida gives to the nonpresence within the presence of the inscription and the letter. "The concept of writing," as he remarks apropos of Rousseau's *Essay on the Origin of Language,* "designates the place of unease [*lieu de malaise*], of the

23. Jacques Derrida, *Speech and Phenomena,* trans. David B. Allison (Evanston, Ill.: Northwestern University Press, 1973), 65.

24. Jacques Derrida, *Edmund Husserl's "Origin of Geometry": An Introduction,* trans. John P. Leavey, Jr. (reprint, Lincoln: University of Nebraska Press, 1989), 92 (translation modified); Edmund Husserl, *L'Origine de la géométrie,* traduction et introduction par Jacques Derrida (Paris: P.U.F., 1962), 90.

regulated incoherence within conceptuality."[25] This uneasy site lies within and beyond the graphite, within and beyond the carbonized remains of the fire; and it opens onto the divisible, unseizable, unthinkable graphematic possibility that lies immeasurably outside even while it leaves its barely discernible graphic trace on the inside. *Verflechtung,* "the supplement," and writing are the names through which Husserl and Rousseau keep a space open for the coming of the other, names through which they at once mark the still withheld essence of language and at the same time attempt to appropriate it for thinking. In these and other readings by Derrida from the 1960s and 1970s one can hear the call of ash and cinders from within the graphic degradation of writing, which in effect already marks out the site of the remains of an absolute outside encrypted on the inside of language.

A "graphics of supplementarity," a "generalized writing," situated, as Derrida writes apropos of the chain of significations at work in Plato's texts, "in the back room [*arrière-boutique*], in the shadows of the pharmacy, prior to the oppositions between conscious and unconscious, freedom and constraint, voluntary and unvoluntary, speech and language."[26] The way to language leads into this back room, and it is here that ash and cinders burn. The essence of language has consumed itself as the condition of the coming to presence of phonic and graphic traces.

Plato's Second Letter concludes with Plato admonishing his correspondent to burn the letter. In the first version of "Plato's Pharmacy" Derrida writes, "reread this letter . . . burn it. And now, to distinguish between two repetitions." Four years later, when the essay was published in *Dissemination,* Derrida made a slight change: "reread this letter . . . burn it. *Il y a là cendre.* And now, to distinguish between two repetitions." Both versions are gathered in the "Animadversions." "Cinders there are" between two repetitions, between the absolute space that

lies beyond the ring and the trace of that other materiality within the ring of empirical space. The other, unnameable materiality was already there, always on the outside, but its traces must also already be on the inside in order for the inside to come to presence. A cinder is what burns in language in lieu of the gift or the promise of the secret of that "first" burning, which may itself be a repetition. Something persists, something keeps ringing and burning between these repetitions; it is this something that gives the strange gift of a cinder.

"Yes, she cried, yes, yes." The thought, the thing that cries here at the end of Maurice Blanchot's *L'Arrêt de mort* (which means at once that which gives death, the "death sentence," and that which stops it, keeps it at bay), is less a phenomenologically identifiable character than it is *la pensée, la chose* that lies within the ashes of the concealed origin of language: "And that now this thing is over there [*là-bas*], now you have unveiled it and, having seen it, you have seen face to face that which lives on for eternity, for yours and for mine!"[27] It is this voice that somehow speaks even within the ashes that Derrida calls *La Cendre,* the Cinder, as in Cendrillon, Cinderella, the one in Perrault's fairy tale who is covered with ashes ("Cucendron," as her nastiest stepsister calls her), the one who remains with the remains of what burns in the hearth. Derrida addresses her throughout *Cinders,* or rather, is addressed by her. " 'Viens,' " writes Blanchot, "et éternellement, elle est là" ("Come," and eternally

25. Jacques Derrida, *Of Grammatology,* trans. Gayatri Chakravorty Spivak (Baltimore: Johns Hopkins University Press, 1976), 237–38; *De la grammatologie* (Paris: Les éditions de Minuit, 1967), 338.

26. Jacques Derrida, "Plato's Pharmacy," in *Dissemination,* trans. Barbara Johnson (Chicago: University of Chicago Press, 1981), 129; *La dissémination* (Paris: Editions de Seuil, 1972), 147.

27. Maurice Blanchot, *Death Sentence,* trans. Lydia Davis (Barrytown, N.Y.: Station Hill, 1978), 79 (translation modified); *L'Arrêt de mort* (Paris: Gallimard, 1948), 125.

she is there). *LA Cendre* is the Other, she affirms the first burning, the first lack (*LAC*), the first "without" that is not really nothing, and she is intertwined, interlaced, an *entrelac,* an interlacing, in the second burning, in all our memories, forgettings, appropriations, and disappropriations.

In *Parages, Ulysse Gramophone,* and several of the essays collected in *Psyche: Inventions de l'autre,* Derrida pursues the issue of the double repetition through readings of Blanchot, Joyce, Michel de Certeau, Heidegger, and others.[28] *Cinders* announces the coming of the "arche-originary *yes*" through the coming of the phrase "Cinders there are," through its double appearance in *Dissemination* and its repetitions and transformations in *Glas* and *The Postcard*. What Derrida in his reading of Joyce calls "the gramophone effect" is another name for the cinder, for the affirmation of the Other in the back room, the Other in the ashes, what Joyce calls the "gramophone in the grave," the automatic, noncognitive writing that preexists the coming of the subject. The essays on Blanchot collected in *Parages* date from 1976 to 1979, while the two essays on Joyce in *Ulysse Gramophone* and the essays on the double "yes" in *Psyche* all follow the publication of *Feu la cendre* in 1982. The coming of the cinder that is the "arche-originary *yes*" is unspoken, inaudible, like the unseizable, unmasterable complex of terms generated in Blanchot's texts by the *pas de . . . , pas-de-nom,* or *pas au-delà,* the nameless step of naming, or the step into an inaccessible beyond. *Là cendre,* with or without the accent, like the *pas de,* signals a pre-originary engagement or commitment, a promise or pledge, that silently binds language to the infinite divisibility of the nonpresent trace, and thus to the Other. In *Of Spirit* Derrida writes *langage* as *l'engage* to indicate our engagement to language as something that precedes all questioning, thinking, and speaking.[29] Cinders are the gage of this engagement, the self-consuming artifacts by which language pledges itself in the very act of immolating the promise it makes. It is the call of the cinder, the coming of *il y a là cendre,* that leads Derrida

from the "graphics of supplementarity" to the thought of the nonpresent Other.

Cinders recounts the *Ereignis* of language that doubles and divides every affirmation, every "yes," placing it between two repetitions, between the Other's silent call and the possibility of Its arrival.

3

This mere word, spaced without space, affirming beneath all affirmation, impossible to deny, too weak to be killed, too docile to be contained, not saying anything, only speaking, speaking without living, without voice, in a voice lower than any voice.

MAURICE BLANCHOT, L'Attente l'oubli

Derrida makes explicit what is merely implicit in Heidegger when it is a question of the intimacy and the remoteness of the Other, which also involves the question of the gender of the Other. She, the grammatical "she," *la cendre,* is "eternally there," which is to say, "eternally nonpresent." The cinder is also at times "he." As Derrida remarks in his essay on the gender of Dasein in *Being and Time,* "one must think of a pre-differential, rather a pre-dual, sexuality," which situates sexual difference at an indeterminate point in the disseminal throw through which Dasein enters spatiality.[30] Dasein's relation to the body is put into question throughout *Cinders*.

28. Jacques Derrida, *Parages* (Paris: Galilée, 1986); *Ulysse Gramophone* (Paris: Galilée, 1987); *Psyche: Inventions de l'autre.* Two essays of particular relevance to the problem of the double repetition have been translated: "Ulysses Gramophone: Hear say yes in Joyce," trans. Tina Kendall, in *James Joyce: The Augmented Ninth,* ed. Bernard Benstock (Syracuse: Syracuse University Press, 1988), 27–75; "A Number of Yes," trans. Brian Holmes, in *Qui Parle* 2 (Fall 1988): 118–33.

29. Derrida, *Of Spirit,* n.5, 129–36.

30. Jacques Derrida, "Geschlecht: Sexual Difference, Ontological Difference," *Research in Phenomenology* 13 (1983): 72, 78–79.

We might also think of the cinder as the "friend" of whom Heidegger speaks: "Hearing constitutes the primary and authentic way in which Dasein is open [*Offenheit*] for its ownmost potentiality-for-Being – as in hearing the voice of the friend whom every Dasein carries with it [*der Stimme des Freundes, den jedes Dasein bei sich trägt*]."[31] Dasein carries her/him, the cinder, the intimate and yet unspeakably remote friend, whose "pre-dual sexuality" (a kind of potentiality for gender) always accompanies the particular gender of a body in real space. Dasein *is* Dasein only insofar as the cinder is there; only insofar as Dasein hears the silent voice of the cinder can Dasein come to the word. S/he keeps her(him)self a secret while s/he lies within our most intimate interiority.

The cinder is not the word, it is not the letter, but what precedes it; and what precedes the letter has already been burned. The cinder comes in lieu of a preoriginary letter that would assure that a letter always reaches its destination, which would be to believe that the letter as language's essence could be made present, could be given, to thought. The remains of a cinder prevent thinking and naming from reaching back before the fire: "this double gesture, to propose a philosophy of cinders and to show how 'cinders' prevent philosophy from closing upon itself."[32] The cinder is neither an entity, nor Being, nor non-Being. Cinders remain of what lies beyond the ring, remain of what is not and was never in the world. The cinder is the dispatch or *envoi* whose incineration makes a letter possible.

But what separates a cinder from an *envoi* and from the other names for the structure of the trace is its evocation of the fire. The title *Feu la cendre* indicates, by virtue of its double displacement of the two meanings of *feu,* yet a further connection – to mourning: "fire," but also "deceased" or "departed." Among the options for a more literal translation are "Fire, Cinder," "Burn the Cinder," or "The Late Cinder," "The Bereaved Cinder," in the archaic sense of "bereaved" as "separated" or "taken away." *Feu* is a homonym of *fut,* and echoes *fût*: fire

burning within the *passé défini* of the verb "to be," within *l'être/lettre*. These echoes are elaborated in an essay from 1977 called "Cartouches," which is about the artwork of Titus Carmel. *Cinders,* like Titus Carmel's matchbox coffins, is a "cartouche," a cinder container bearing the phrase *il y a là cendre,* a cinder *envoi* that is also an explosive cartridge (also *cartouche* in French), that commemorates the "firepower" of a nonpresent (divine) name, an exploded paradigm: "the suicide paradigm retrac(t)ing by blowing itself up. It scuttles [*saborde*]. *Fuit* [in Latin, 'it was'; in French, 'flees' or 'fled'] the former model. *Feu (sur) le paradigme* [fire on the paradigm; the late paradigm]. *Il-fût.*"[33] *Feu la cendre* takes this structure of aesthetic autodestruction to its inevitable limits, where the contents of the cartouche, the phrase itself, autodestructs: "a self-destructive virtue firing on its own right into the heart." From *feu le paradigme* to *feu la cendre,* from the deconstruction of aesthetic judgment to that of ontology. The cartouche and the cinder call upon us to mourn the lack of paradigms and holy names. But what is it to mourn the disappearance of something that was never present?

In a brief essay entitled "Transience" (*Vergänglichkeit*) (1916)[34] Freud recounts a conversation he had with a friend and a young poet whose "aching despondency" concerning the transience of earthly beauty was unaffected by Freud's argument

31. Martin Heidegger, *Being and Time,* trans. John Macquarrie and Edward Robinson (New York: Harper & Row, 1962), 163.

32. Didier Cahen, "Vers la déconstruction: Entretien avec Jacques Derrida," *Digraphe* 42 (1987): 24. My translation.

33. Jacques Derrida, *The Truth in Painting,* trans. Geoff Bennington and Ian MacLeod (Chicago: University of Chicago Press, 1987), 229. Translation slightly modified. Is not the fiery breath of Heraclitean *phusis* strangely (in)audible here?

34. Sigmund Freud, "On Transience," in *The Standard Edition of the Complete Psychological Works of Sigmund Freud,* ed. James Strachey, 24 vols. (London: Hogarth Press and the Institute of Psycho-Analysis, 1957), 14:303–7.

that transience in fact only lends things greater charm. Freud's failure to persuade his companions suggests to him that they are influenced by "some powerful emotional factor" which he calls "a foretaste of mourning" (*einen Vorgeschmack der Trauer*). In *Glas* and *Fors* Derrida elaborates on the orality of the mourning process and on its connection to the introjection and incorporation of words, phonemes, and letters. For Derrida there is no introjection without incorporation, no idealization of the one who is departed that does not leave some unassimilable residue behind, some piece or fragment of the other or the other's speech secretly lodged or incorporated within the mourner's speech or behavior. This is also the case with language as such: we cannot take it in without also coming upon the unassimilable remains of the Other. It is this otherness of the word that Derrida calls the "bit," or *mors*, as in the "piece," or *morceau*, of the dead that one eats in a cannibalistic mourning ritual, a ritual that is in effect enacted whenever one comes to the word, for whenever one inhales or exhales the vocable, one also eats a piece of the word's otherness, of the departed Other it silently bears with it. To come to the word is incessantly to taste these cinder remains. Freud's concern in "Transience" is with the temporality of things, with one's mournful "foretaste" of "temporal limitation" (*zeitliche Beschränkung*). What makes mourning such "a great enigma" (*großes Rätsel*) is the pain caused by the "detachment" (*Ablösung*) of libido from the lost object: "We see only that libido clings [*klammert*] to its objects and will not renounce those that are lost even when a substitute lies ready to hand." It is the cinder beyond the word, other than the word, that nevertheless clings to the word, that is sprinkled on it and that burns within it. Mourning ends when "it has consumed itself" (*sich selbst aufgezehrt*) by eventually renouncing its former attachments. Derrida is interested in what persists within the "enigma" of mourning, of what still "clings," what still continues to burn and cannot be consumed. For Derrida mourning always entails melancholia, an infinite attenuation of the clinging to something "there." Freud writes in "Mourning and Melancholia" that both normal and melancholic mourning share the "characteristic of detaching the libido bit by bit" (*Einzeldurchführung*).[35] Derrida's name for this attenuated clinging is borrowed from the nineteenth-century convention of *demi-deuil,* the "half" or "partial mourning" that follows "high mourning." For Derrida we are always already in half mourning, for there is no end to the "bit by bit" divisibility of a cinder. Pushing still further Abraham's linguistic elaboration of Imre Hermann's study of libidinal clinging (*cramponnement*),[36] Derrida discovers the clinging to language of something beyond language: the clinging of the bit, the *mors,* which is also of course the *mort,* the dead. What in *Glas* Derrida calls the *effet de mors,* the "bit-" or "death-effect," the effect of the *gl* (as in glottis), the *cl*inging, sticky work of the tongue that at once makes possible and resists absolutely all idealization and conceptualization,[37] this *call* of something entirely other from within the silent ringing of *glas,* takes in *Cinders* the form of a "raw cinder, that is more to his taste."

But there is still something more to this name among others that is a cinder. *Cinders* "would tell of the all-burning, otherwise called holocaust and the crematory oven, in German in all the Jewish languages of the world." The work as cartouche commemorates "an impossible tomb"; it constitutes "the memory of a cenotaph," an inscription on an empty tomb.

When Hegel writes in *Phenomenology of Spirit* and *Lectures on the Philosophy of Religion* of the torrents of fire and light, of the

---

35. Freud, "Mourning and Melancholia," in *The Standard Edition,* 14:256.

36. Cf. Imre Hermann, *L'Instinct filial,* introduction by Nicolas Abraham (Paris: Denoël, 1972).

37. *Glas,* 235b.

"streams of fire destructive of [all] structured form,"[38] he calls the coming of the all-burning light of sunrise a "sacrifice" (*Opfer*) in which the Being-for-itself of spirit burns itself, consumes itself in order to preserve itself. Derrida suggests in *Glas* that "holocaust" is a better translation of *Opfer* than "sacrifice" and indeed that "holocaust" (all [*holos*] is burned [*caustos*]) is a more appropriate word for the process Hegel describes than *Opfer* itself. Derrida's holocaust means something different, however, than Hegel's *Opfer*. In Hegel's speculative dialectic the holocaust is spirit's gift of itself to itself; its excursion into what Hegel calls its "otherness" only insures its return to itself. For Hegel, writes Derrida, "The gift can only be a sacrifice, that is the axiom of speculative reason. Even if it upsurges 'before' philosophy and religion, the gift has for its destination or determination, for its *Bestimmung*, a return to self in philosophy, religion's truth."[39] Hegel's sacrificial holocaust makes the otherness of the holocaust itself *appear*, it pretends to bring it to presence, while Derrida's holocaust remains entirely other, nonpresent and outside the theorizable limits of ontology, leaving only the cinder traces of an absolute nonmemory. It is the *non*-sacrificial nature of the Nazi Extermination that is silently at stake throughout the section of *Glas* that forms the central and longest section of the "Animadversions." A certain continuity is thus also (and still silently) sketched between Hegel's sacrificial logic, which ontologized the essence of unhiddenness, and the aesthetic or cathartic motivation of the Nazi Extermination, the most monstrous gift of appropriation, which sought to purge Europe of its unaesthetic inhabitants, Jews above all, but also dissidents and eccentrics of all sorts – political, sexual, or cultural; "of the others," writes Derrida, "cinder there is."

Cinders resist the domination of the essence of unhiddenness by the dialectic, by mind, reason, spirit, etc. In so doing, they eliminate the possibility of the anniversary, the return back to

itself, of spirit, energy, will, form, etc. Can we think the otherness of what is outside the ring, think of it as something that can never come back to itself? Thinking what Derrida calls "the time of a cinder" denies us the consolation of "the logic of the anniversary, the imposition of the curve on the angle."[40] It means thinking the ring's displacement from itself, "dispersion without return," a truly "pyromaniac dissemination." One thus commemorates a cinder's not-belonging to itself, another kind of anniversary, the anniversary of an absolute nonmemory, the ringing together of what no longer takes the shape of a circle.

Mourning, ashes, the holocaust, the breathing in and eating of the remains of cinders, the anniversary, the ring, the absolute singularity of the date, these elements of *Cinders* all signal the pervasive influence of Paul Celan. In *Schibboleth: Pour Paul Celan* we read: "Il y a la cendre, peut-être, mais une cendre n'est pas" (There are cinders, perhaps, but a cinder is not). The passage continues: "This remainder *seems* to remain of what was [*fut*], and what was [*fut*] just now; it seems to feed or drink from the source of being-present, but it comes out of being, it uses up in advance the being on which it seems to draw. The remnant of the remainder – the cinder, almost nothing – is not a being that remains, if at least one understands here a being that subsists." This passage is by way of a reading of Celan's "Mit der Aschenkelle geschöpft" (Drawn with the ladle of cinders / from the trough of Being): "What is drawn, inhaled, drunk (*geschöpft*) with the ladle (*Kelle*; the source or the fountain, *Quelle*, is not far), with the ladle of cinders, with the cinder spoon (*mit der Aschenkelle*), comes out of the trough of Be-

38. G.W.F. Hegel, *Phenomenology of Spirit*, trans. A. V. Miller (Oxford: Oxford University Press, 1977), 419.

39. *Glas*, 243a.

40. *Glas*, 245a.

ing (*aus dem Seinstrog*)."[41] The cinder ladle comes out of Being *seifig,* soapy, slippery, a slippery cinder, nearest the source of Being but most difficult to grasp. The process by which the cinder serves up the word describes the central scene of Celan's writing: the coming again and again of the cinder that bears the word, and that, in bearing the word, consumes it. Derrida's holocaust is identical with the radical nonidentity of the ringing of an anniversary in Celan:

Consumption, becoming a cinder, conflagration or incineration of a date: on the hour, in the hour itself, every hour. It is the threat of an absolute crypt: the non-return, the unreadability, the amnesia without remainder, but the non-return as return, *in* the return itself. *[. . .] There is certainly today a date for this holocaust that we know, the hell of our memory; but there is a holocaust for every date, somewhere in the world at every hour.*[42]

The ringing of this anniversary cuts into the word, incises the ring at an an*gle,* circumcises the word (which is Derrida's leitmotif in *Schibboleth*): "circumcision of the word by the incision of the nothing in the circumcised heart of the other, that's you," that's the cinder, the friend of uncertain gender who always accompanies Dasein.[43] All languages are Jewish in this sense, consumed by the cinder that bears them and burns them from within, by the all-burning oven named in the Greek *holokaustos* "in German in all the Jewish languages of the world."

4

How is it called, your land
behind mountains, behind years?

PAUL CELAN, "Es ist alles anders"

Celan's oblique presence in *Cinders* is one of the most finely nuanced inflections by which Derrida defines his own neighborhood of poetic naming and thoughtful saying. The cassette recording that accompanies the 1987 French edition, in which

the author and Carole Bouquet read *Feu la cendre* with the occasional accompaniment of Stockhausen's hauntingly ethereal *Stimmung,* brings the question of thinking and poetry directly to bear upon what Derrida calls the "polylogue," "an unpronounceable conversation," between the audible sonority of the indeterminate number of voices of *Cinders* and the still silent voice, the absolutely minimal voice of the Other. "But how," asks Derrida, "can this fatally silent call that speaks before its own voice be made audible?" The various tonalities and moods of voice, already marked in the written text and still more discernible in the recorded version, succeed in making the inaudible call of the Other yet more discernible, by always calling, in all their multiplicity and gender confusion, for yet another voice, for one that would bring us still closer to the "you" that speaks in a cinder. Cinderella is one name among others for the still withheld essence of the cinder friend that is borne along with Dasein. By varying the intonation, by trying to mark or to efface the *accent grave* in *là cendre* (which sometimes even looks like an anagram of *ce(la)n*), the spoken voices begin, as Derrida remarks, to say something about "the experience of cinders and song." The song of poetic saying would thus sing to and of the inaudible, nonpresent incineration that burns within every experience: "this experience of incineration that is experience itself."[44] We can only think the otherness of the other's inaudible voice, but our thinking about it is always inseparable from poetic saying, from the audible song, prayer, or hymn that would bring us as close as possible to the silence in which the voice of the Other burns. *Cinders* is situated in the neighborhood of this haunted crossing, in the nearness of the *khorismos,* near what Derrida calls "the absolute hiatus."

41. Derrida, *Schibboleth: Pour Paul Celan,* 77. My translation.

42. *Schibboleth,* 83. My translation.

43. *Schibboleth,* 110. My translation.

44. Cahen, "Vers la déconstruction," 23.

The neighborhood of *Dichten* and *Denken* is convened by the Other's silent call. "But poetic saying that thinks [*das denkende Dichten*]," writes Heidegger, "is in truth / the topology of Being [*Seyns*]."[45] Such saying, Heidegger continues, "tells [*sagt*] Being the habitation [*Ortschaft*] of its essence [*Wesens*]," its still concealed essence. Being comes into the proximity of poetic saying and thinking and thus establishes and signals its topology, the place it has come to inhabit, the place (*Ort*) that is distinct from space (*Raum*). This is what occurs in the coming of the phrase *il y a là cendre,* the phrase that establishes and signals a place (*il y a lieu* / Place there is), a place that is not to be conceived or experienced spatially. What Derrida calls the "locality" (*le paysage*) of "cinders there are" suggests the habitation or topology of a cinder that is evoked in the words *Ortschaft* and *Nachbarschaft.* The neighborhood of poetic saying and thinking is a place or site that belongs to the topology of another spatiality which Derrida and Heidegger (re)name and (re)think throughout their writing. The specific modalities of the naming and thinking of that neighborhood point to important resemblances and differences between Heidegger and Derrida which bear significantly upon the tonality of *il y a là cendre*.

Là cendre names the persistent concealment of Dasein's essence, indeed it translates that concealment into French; *là-cendre* at once translates and reconfigures *da-Sein*. Like Dasein a cinder lies within the difference of the unextended space of the *res cogitans* or "thinking thing" and the extended space of the *res extensa,* within the *différance* between the intelligible and the sensible; it is what makes cognition possible while withholding itself from representation or conceptualization. A cinder lies finally on the far side of Dasein, just beyond the edge of its Being-in-the-world. It thus follows the trajectory of Heidegger's effort to name and think the word that would bring to presence, that would distance and "un-distance" (*ent-fernen*) the "region" (*Gegend*) in which Being comes to language. By situating the places in language where Being comes to reside, such naming and thinking bring Being into the audible range of beings who can thus be called into their own. To discover these traces, grooves, and effractions in language through which Being marks its silent withdrawal is to come to the liminal threshold of the site of this other spatiality that is composed of another materiality, a spatiality into which three-dimensional space and time emerge, and that, in gathering together and sustaining the differences between past, present, and future, would constitute another temporal or extratemporal dimension. Heidegger asks us to think of the concealed origin of language as being situated on this dimensional cusp. His later thinking searches, listens, and lingers within language for traces of what in *Being and Time* he called Dasein's capacity to "take space in," or to "break into space." Instead of asking how Dasein could enter time-space, the later Heidegger asks what it is that enables time-space to get underway. Moving from the near to the far side of the ontological difference, moving from Dasein to language, Heidegger seems at times to write as though the final, absolutely literal proper name for the materiality of this other space-time were near to hand, as though it were on the verge of becoming palpable.

What in *Being and Time* he calls the "spiritual" (*geistig*) essence of Dasein's ability to become spatial,[46] belies a profound commitment to the possibility of such naming. As Derrida demonstrates in *Of Spirit, Geist* names, in early and late Heidegger,

45. Martin Heidegger, "The Thinker as Poet," in *Poetry, Language, Thought,* trans. Albert Hofstadter (New York: Harper & Row, 1971), 12 (translation modified); *Aus der Erfahrung des Denkens,* Bd. 13 of *Gesamtausgabe,* ed. Hermann Heidegger (Frankfurt am Main: Vittorio Klostermann, 1983), 84.

46. "Neither may Dasein's spatiality be interpreted as an imperfection which adheres to existence by reason of the fatal 'linkage of the spirit to a body.' On the contrary, because Dasein is 'spiritual,' *and only because of this,* it can be spatial in a way that remains essentially impossible for any extended corporeal thing," *Being and Time,* 368.

the site of the proximity of Being's proper name, the site of fire and ashes. Whereas in *Being and Time* it is the spiritual (*geistig*) essence of Dasein's "ecstatical-horizontal temporality" that enables it to break into space, in "Language in the Poem" that essence burns within the mystery of ghostly or *geistlich* fire. Spirit as fire leads Heidegger closer to that other materiality than had spirit as the breath of mind and thought. Rejecting the *geistig* thinking of Platonism and Christianity, as well as his own earlier celebration of the *geistig* force of Dasein and the German people, Heidegger, in a gesture whose intemperate impatience Derrida devastatingly reveals, turns to Trakl's *geistlich* land: "This land is older, which is to say, earlier and therefore more promising [*versprechender*] than the Platonic-Christian land, or indeed than a land conceived in terms of the European West. For apartness is the 'first beginning' of a mounting world-year, not the abyss of decay."[47] Heidegger wants to come as close as he can to the fire of the promise that burns within language, always closer to the inmost materiality of the fire. His advocacy of Dasein's *geistig* essence during the 1930s had, perhaps inadvertently, provided cover for the forces of destruction. Perhaps the haunting return of *Geist* in its fiery, *geistlich* guise would lead, not to the decay of a decomposing *Geschlecht*, but to the "mounting world-year" of "one flesh."

This "more promising" beginning, whatever its salutary utopian possibility, involves a promise no less impossible than the erstwhile promise of its *geistig* predecessor. Invoking the memorable and ineluctable wrinkle which Paul de Man introduced into Heidegger's famous formula, *Die Sprache spricht* (language speaks), Derrida remarks that de Man's *Die Sprache verspricht sich* addresses precisely the problem that Heidegger's differentiation of *Geist* has led him into:

Language or speech promises, promises itself but also goes back on its word, becomes undone or unhinged, derails or becomes delirious, deteriorates, becomes corrupt just as immediately and just as essentially. It cannot not promise as soon as it speaks, it is promise, but it cannot fail to break its promise – and this comes of the structure of the promise, as of the event it nonetheless institutes.[48]

This deterioration, this fragility of language, this degradation at the heart of language, is something Heidegger everywhere confronts only to turn away from it at the last moment. Heidegger wants to think of *Geist* at its most essential as being somehow free of the decomposition of human generation, while Derrida's deconstructive reading shows that the most *versprechende* beginning is nevertheless heir to the corruption of language.

Cinders name this corruption, they anticipate language's inevitable crumblings and deteriorations. Though, arguably, no one has understood better than Heidegger the delicacy of language and its susceptibility to breakdowns and misfires, denials and negations, indeed the entire network of terms and ideas that can be generated from *versagen*, this understanding is invariably placed in the service of an even more profound susceptibility to the lure of the finally proper name.[49] *Cinders*, however, plays with the tormenting will to speak the proper name. Derrida plays with the deadly serious proximity and distance of the fire that burns and subsides within a language. The "continuous, tormenting, obsessive meditation about what are and are not, what is meant – or silenced by, cinders" moves incessantly from mourning to telepathy, from the most impossible distance to the most unbearable proximity. Derrida's cinders

47. Heidegger, *On the Way to Language*, 194 (*Unterwegs*, 77).

48. Derrida, *Of Spirit*, 93–94. Also see Derrida's discussion of de Man's *Die Sprache verspricht sich* in *Memoires: For Paul de Man*, trans. Cecile Lindsay, Jonathan Culler, and Eduardo Cadava (New York: Columbia University Press, 1986), 94–101.

49. I have indicated some of these crossings, which result in a certain overpowering of *Dichten* by *Denken*, in my essay "Writing on Ashes: Heidegger *Fort Derrida*," *Diacritics* 19.3–4 (1989): 128–48.

cannot escape or overcome the promise of, and the desire for, the literal name, but by anticipating the broken promise, by remaining alert to the trope lurking within every concept and the concept concealed within every trope, they inject a certain restless instability that may make it inevitable as well as necessary that we constantly invent new versions of the Other and thus of the others.

Language rises like a wave out of its unthinkable origin and comes into the linguistic habitations (the *Ortschaft*) of human speech or into the *Gedicht* of the poet. It is up to thinkers to make these habitations audible, and up to poets to discover the song within these traces. The rising itself is a silent ringing, a hissing noise, like heat escaping, like something burning, a wave of agitated motion which thinkers and poets translate into differing modes of audibility. As this wave rises from its impossible distance, mourning becomes telepathy, and we receive what Derrida calls "the impossible emission." *Tele-pathos,* the transmission over a distance of the Other's state of being, the ability to feel the heat of the Other, is more properly speaking *tele-kaustos,* the sending of what burns within a cinder. *Telekaustos* would mean, not thought-transference, but the transference of that other materiality within thought which at once sustains thought and withholds itself from thought. The opening of another topology through language is the work of *telekaustos,* the sending of a cinder signal.

Early and late Heidegger succumbed to the persuasive power of *Geist*. And early and late in his writing there is a clearly defined sacrificial logic. In order to define perhaps the most significant feature of *Cinders,* let us consider a characteristic instance of Heidegger's understanding of the relation between "historical being" and the advent of the essential thinking that thinks the truth of Being:

The thinking whose thoughts not only do not calculate but are really [überhaupt] *determined by what is Other than beings* [dem Anderen des Seienden] *is called essential thinking. Rather than count on beings with beings, it expends itself in Being for the truth of Being. This thinking answers to the demands of Being in that man surrenders* [überantwortet] *his historical being to the simple, sole necessity whose constraints do not so much necessitate as create the need which is fulfilled in the freedom of the sacrifice* [Freiheit des Opfers].[50]

It is through one's courage to make the sacrifice, Heidegger continues, that one enters into "the neighborhood of the indestructible." The thinker's "saying" of Being and the poet's "naming of the holy" seek, in their distinct ways, "to care for" the words in which Being's "soundless voice" rings. This statement of the sacrificial logic underlying the neighborhood of *Dichten* and *Denken,* which Heidegger wrote in 1943, makes explicit the fundamental content of Heidegger's thinking before and after. Sacrifice entails that we must reconfigure our historical being once we have entered into relation with the truth of Being, even if that truth is still only the trace of something lacking and withheld. There would be nothing particularly alarming about such a scenario were it not for the fact that Heidegger's "essential thinking" lavishes itself, indeed squanders itself (*verschwendet sich*) on the truth of Being. This is how he had endorsed the *geistig* essence of German Dasein, and how he will endorse the coming of a *geistlich* epoch in his later writing. There is nothing left for historical being but the prospect of its imminent cessation as the logic of sacrifice bears essential thinking ever closer to the fire of the spirit.

The disengagement of Heidegger's thinking from the sacrificial logic underlying it has been an important part of Derrida's

50. Martin Heidegger, "Postscript" to *What is Metaphysics?* in *Existence and Being,* ed. Werner Brock (Chicago: Henry Regnery, 1949), 357–58 (translation modified); "Nachwort zu 'Was ist Metaphysik'," in *Wegmarken,* Bd.9 of *Gesamtausgabe,* ed. Friedrich-Wilhelm von Hermann (Frankfurt am Main: Vittorio Klostermann, 1976), 309.

thinking early and late. Derrida recognized very early that the only way to enable essential thinking to reconfigure historical being was to remove it from the logic of sacrifice. The relation between logic and sacrifice is of the utmost importance here, for it is Heidegger's intention to mark an absolute break between logic, or "calculative thought," and sacrifice, which involves our submission to those prelogical thoughts that "are absolutely [*überhaupt*] determined by what is 'Other' than what-is." Heidegger insists that "sacrifice tolerates [*duldet*] no calculation, for calculation always miscalculates [*verrechnet*] sacrifice in terms of the expedient and the inexpedient."[51] It has always been clear to Derrida that Heidegger's sacrifice on behalf of the Other provides cover for the most calculating ideological and psychological investments. Heidegger's sacrifice to the Other lends itself too readily to a calculated sacrifice of the others who do not appear to share the experience of essential thinking. Heidegger even calls the sacrifice "the departure from beings [*Abschied vom Seienden*]." While for Heidegger "calculation disfigures [*verunstaltet*] the nature of sacrifice," for Derrida the insurmountability of miscalculation and disfiguration exposes the dangers of the surreptitious logic of sacrifice. Derrida reveals the secret economy of loss and gain that sustains even the sublime fiction of a sacrifice *à fond perdu.*

She, the Cinder, blocks the path of Heidegger's impossible sacrifice. Heidegger would risk everything on the withheld origin of the "call of conscience" that comes from Dasein's innermost essence, from the being "there."[52] Derrida wants only to take a chance on the Other, to reveal that no sacrifice will succeed in bringing the Other to presence, and to acknowledge that the experience of a cinder describes our *ethos,* our "dwelling-place" as human beings. Derrida listens more closely than Heidegger and discerns the almost inaudible call of the Cinder, its strange androgynous intonation. Derrida's recognition or acknowledgement of our debt to the Other purges Heidegger's thinking of its Romantic apocalypticism and thus provides us with a realistic basis on which to rethink and reinvent our relations to others. Though it is not yet present and may never be present, the place of the Other is nevertheless real, and through it we can deconstruct the transcendent idealities and materialities that pretend to bring it to presence.

Cinders is the *for intérieur* of Derrida's oeuvre, where he hears the "lack" that comes like a whisper from the far side of Dasein, from the distant entity beyond Being that holds everything in Being. *Cinders* recounts the emergence of conscience as the recognition of our debt to the Other and to the others. "That is what is owed to the fire, and yet, if possible, without the shadow of a sacrifice." These words from *Cinders* may provide the best clue to translating the enigma of *il y a là cendre.*

51. *Existence and Being,* 359 (translation modified); *Wegmarken,* 311.

52. *Being and Time,* 317–25.

Prologue

Il y a plus de 15 ans, une phrase m'est venue, comme malgré moi, revenue plutôt, singulière, singulièrement brève, presque muette.

Je la croyais savamment calculée maîtrisée, assujettie, comme si je me l'étais à tout jamais appropriée.

Or depuis, sans cesse je dois me rendre à l'évidence: la phrase s'était passé de toute autorisation, elle avait vécu sans moi.

Elle avait toujours vécu seule.

La première fois (était-ce la première fois?), ce fut donc il y a plus de 15 ans, à la fin d'un livre, *La dissémination.* Dans un paragraphe de remerciements, au moment où un livre se dédicace, se donne ou se rend à ceux qui, connus ou inconnus, vous l'ont d'avance donné ladite phrase vient s'imposer à moi avec l'autorité, si discrète et simple qu'elle fût, d'une sentence: *il y a là cendre.*

Là s'écrivait avec un accent grave: *là,* il y a cendre, il y a, *là,* cendre. Mais l'accent, s'il se lit à l'œil, ne s'entend pas: il y a là cendre. A l'écoute, l'article défini, *la,* risque d'effacer le lieu, la mention ou la mémoire du lieu, l'adverbe là . . . Mais à la lecture muette, c'est l'inverse, *là* efface *la, la* s'efface: lui-même, elle-même, deux fois plutôt qu'une.

Cette phrase, dont chaque lettre en secret comptait pour moi, je l'ai ensuite reprise, citation ou non, dans d'autres textes: *Glas, La carte postale,* par exemple.

More than 15 years ago a phrase came to me, as though in spite of me; to be more precise, it returned, unique, uniquely succinct, almost mute.

I thought I had calculated it cunningly, mastered and overwhelmed it, as if I had appropriated it once and for all.

Since then, I have repeatedly had to yield to the evidence: the phrase dispensed with all authorization, she had lived without me.

She, the phrase, had always lived alone.

The first time (was it the first time?), more than 15 years ago, at the end of a book, *Dissemination,* in the acknowledgments, where a book is dedicated, offered, rendered up to those who, known or unknown, have already given it to you in advance, the sentence in question imposed itself upon me with the authority, so discreet and simple it was, of a judgment: "cinders there are" (*il y a là cendre*).

Là written with an accent *grave*: *là,* there, cinder there is, there is, there, cinder. But the accent, although readable to the eye, is not heard: cinder there is. To the ear, the definite article, *la,* risks effacing the place, and any mention or memory of the place, the adverb *là* . . . But read silently, it is the reverse: *là* effaces *la, la* effaces herself, himself, twice rather than once.

This sentence, in which each letter had a secret meaning for me, I used again later, whether a citation or not, in other texts: *Glas, The Postcard,* for example.

Pendant près de dix ans, allées et venues de ce spectre, visites inopinées du revenant. La chose parlait toute seule. Je devais m'expliquer avec elle, lui répondre – ou en répondre.

Quand des amis, en 1980, m'ont invité à écrire sur le thème de la cendre pour une revue qui a maintenant disparu, *Anima,* j'ai proposé, dans le genre parodié du polylogue, une conversation apparemment imprononçable, en vérité un dispositif d'écritures qui, pourrait-on dire, *faisait appel* à la voix, à des voix. Mais comment faire entendre cet appel fatalement silencieux qui parle avant sa propre voix? Comment le laisser attendre?

Sur la page, en effet, deux écrits se font face: d'une part, à droite, le polylogue proprement dit, un enchevêtrement de voix en nombre indéterminé, dont certaines paraissent masculines, d'autres féminines, et cela se marque parfois dans la grammaire de la phrase. Ces signes grammaticaux sont lisibles mais ils disparaissent pour la plupart à l'audition, ce qui aggrave une certaine indécision entre l'écriture et la voix, indécision dont le mot *là,* avec ou sans accent, dans *il y a là cendre,* faisait déjà courir le risque.

Cette tension risquée entre l'écriture et la parole, cette vibration de la grammaire à la voix, c'est aussi l'un des thèmes du polylogue. Celui-ci semble-t-il, se destinait à l'œil, il ne s'accordait qu'à la voix intérieure, une voix absolument basse.

For nearly ten years, this specter's comings and goings, unforeseen visits of the ghost. The thing spoke all on its own. I had to explain myself to it, respond to it – or for it.

When some friends, in 1980, invited me to write on the theme of cinders for *Anima,* a now defunct journal, I proposed, in the parodied genre of the polylogue, an apparently unpronounceable conversation, really a writing apparatus that, one might say, *called* to the voice, to voices. But how can this fatally silent call that speaks before its own voice be made audible? How could it be kept waiting any longer?

In effect two pieces of writing come face to face on the page: on the righthand side, the polylogue proper, an entanglement of an indeterminate number of voices, of which some seem masculine, others feminine, and this is sometimes marked in the grammar of the sentence. These readable grammatical signs disappear for the most part when spoken aloud, which aggravates a certain indecision between writing and voice, an indecision already risked by the word *là,* with or without the accent, in "cinders *there* are" [*il y a là cendre*].

This tension risked between writing and speech, this vibration of grammar in the voice, is one of the themes of the polylogue. And this polylogue, it seems, is destined for the eye; it corresponds only to an interior voice, an absolutely low voice.

Mais par là même il donnait à lire, il analysait peut-être ce qu'une mise en voix pouvait appeler et à la fois menacer de perdre, une profération impossible et des tonalités introuvables. Oserai-je dire de mon désir qu'il avait lieu, son lieu, entre cet appel et cette menace? Qu'attendait-il?

Vint un jour la possibilité, il faut dire la chance de cette gramophonie. Avant d'être technique (ce qu'elle est aussi à un moment d'innovation singulière dans l'histoire de l'édition), cette chance suppose le désir, ici celui d'Antoinette Fouque: frayer le passage à ces voix qui travaillent une écriture au corps. Et en somme les mettre en œuvre, enfin à l'œuvre. Non pour substituer la scène vocale au livre, mais pour donner à l'une et à l'autre, l'une et l'autre s'affectant ou se relançant ainsi, leur espace ou plutôt leur volume *respectif:* je ne crois pas que la lecture silencieuse en souffre, ni le désir du livre, au contraire, il reçoit de cette expérience de nouvelles puissances interpétatives. Les éditions *Des femmes* ne proposent pas seulement ce double médium, la page et le volume sonore, désormais indissociables dans leur hétérogénéité même, elles donnent son lieu à une sorte de laboratoire d'études, un studio des écritures vocales, dans lequel une expérience de l'interprétation devient possible.

A quelle expérimentation nous sommes-nous donc livrés ensemble, Michèle Muller, Carole Bouquet et moi-même?

But precisely thereby [*par là*] the polylogue engaged reading; it analyzed perhaps what vocalization [*mise en voix*] could call forth and at the same time risk losing, an impossible utterance and undiscoverable tonalities. Will I dare to say that my desire had a place, its place, between this call and this risk. What was it waiting for?

Then one day came the possibility, I should say the chance of making a tape-recording of this. Before the technical means (which themselves mark a moment of singular innovation in the history of publishing), this opportunity presupposes the desire, here that of Antoinette Fouque: to breach a way into the voices at work in a body of writing. And in short, to situate them in the work, indeed to put them to work. Not in order to substitute the vocal setting for the book, but to give to each of them their space or rather their *specific* volume, in such a way that each medium is affected or reinvented by the other. I do not believe that silent reading will suffer from this, nor the book's desire, which, on the contrary, receives new interpretive impetus from this experiment. *Des Femmes* proposes not only this double medium, printed page and tape recording, from here on indissociable in their very heterogeneity, but also provides a place for it, a sort of research laboratory, a *studio* of vocal writing, in which an interpretive experiment becomes possible.

On what experiment have we embarked together, Michèle Muller, Carole Bouquet and myself? We have

Nous avons mis à l'épreuve cette question – à la fois une peur et un défi: à quelles conditions risquer l'acte de haute voix, celui-là même que j'avais attendu, mais d'avance décrit, annoncé, redouté surtout comme l'impossible même, d'autres diraient *l'interdit?* Car sur la page, c'est comme si chaque mot était choisi puis placé de telle sorte qu'aucune profération par aucune voix jamais n'y accède.

Dans certains cas, en l'absence d'exigences marquées et contradictoires, c'est l'indétermination même qui rendait périlleux le passage à l'acte gramophonique: trop de liberté, mille façons, toutes aussi légitimes, d'accentuer, de marquer le rythme, de faire varier le ton.

Dans d'autres cas, qu'il s'agisse encore de césure, de pause ou d'accord, les décisions les plus contradictoires étaient simultanément requises: la même syllabe *doit* être prononcée sur des registres *incompatibles*. Et donc ne le doit pas. Cette potentialité peut rester, si on peut dire, dans le fond, et se percevoir à la lecture silencieuse, précisémént, enveloppée, voilée. Comment la faire sortir de sa réserve sans un acte de foi, le hiatus absolu à l'instant d'une décision impossible? Celle-ci se trouve toujours confiée, le moment venu, à la voix de l'autre. Non, à *une* voix de l'autre, à une autre voix: celle, ici, de Carole Bouquet.

put this question to the test – at once fearful and defiant: Under what conditions does one take the risk of vocalization, the very act I had awaited, having already described it, given notice of it, above all dreaded it as the impossible itself, some would say the "prohibited" [*l'interdit*]? On the page it is as though each word were chosen, then placed in such a way that nothing uttered by any voice could gain access to it.

In certain cases, in the absence of indications to the contrary, it is the indetermination itself that makes the experience of the gramophonic act so perilous: too much freedom, a thousand ways, all just as legitimate, to accentuate, to set the rhythm, to make the tone change.

In other cases, where it is still a question of cesura, pause or agreement, the most contradictory decisions were required simultaneously: the same syllable *should* be pronounceable on two *incompatible* registers. But then again it shouldn't be. This potentiality remains, so to speak, in the background [*dans le fond*], to be perceived by silent reading precisely as something enveloped, veiled. How can we force this potentiality out of hiding without an act of faith, the absolute hiatus at the moment of an impossible decision? This decision is always confided, when the time comes, to the other's voice. No, to *a voice* of the other, to another voice: here, that of Carole Bouquet.

Qui décidera si cette voix fut prêtée, rendue ou donnée? Et à qui?

En s'engageant dans les choix impossibles, la haute voix ''recordée'' donne à lire une réserve de l'écriture, ses pulsions tonales et phoniques, les ondes (ni le cri ni la parole) qui se nouent ou dénouent dans l'unique vocifération, la singulière portée d'une autre voix. Celle-ci, à filtrer les possibles, se laisse alors passer, elle est d'avance passée, mémoire doublement présente ou présence dédoublée.

Qu'est-ce qui s'engage dans cet acte phonographique? une interprétation, une seule parmi d'autres. A chaque syllabe, à chaque silence même, une décision s'est imposée: elle ne fut pas toujours délibérée, ni parfois la même d'une répétition à l'autre. Et elle ne signe ni la loi ni la vérité. D'autres interprétations restent possibles — et sans doute nécessaires. On analyse ainsi la ressource que nous offre aujourd'hui ce double texte: un espace graphique d'une part, ouvert à une multiplicité de lectures, dans la forme traditionnelle et sauve du livre — et c'est autre chose qu'un livret puisqu'il est *re-donné* à lire, un autre don, la nouvelle donne d'une première fois; mais d'autre part, simultanément, et aussi pour la première fois, voici l'archive sonore d'une interprétation singulière, un jour, par tel ou telle, calcul et chance d'un seul coup.

A trancher, quelquefois sans le vouloir, entre plusieurs inter-

Who will decide whether this voice was lent, returned, or given? And to whom?

By entangling itself in impossible choices, the spoken "recorded" voice makes a reservoir of writing readable, its tonal and phonic drives, the waves (neither cry nor speech) which are knotted or unknotted in the unique vociferation, the singular range of another voice. This voice, to narrow the possibilities, is then left to pass away, it has passed away in advance, doubly present memory or doubly divided presence.

What is involved in this phonographic act? Here's an interpretation, one among others. At each syllable, even at each silence, a decision is imposed: it was not always deliberate, nor sometimes even the same from one repetition to the other. And what it signs is neither the law nor the truth. Other interpretations remain possible — and doubtless necessary. Thus we analyze the resource this double text affords us today: on the one hand, a graphic space opened to multiple readings, in the traditional and protected form of the book — and it is not like a libretto, because each time it gives a different reading, another gift, dealing out a new hand all over again — but on the other hand, simultaneously, and also for the first time, we have the tape recording of a singular interpretation, made one day, by so on and so forth, at a single stroke calculated and by chance.

To decide, sometimes without wanting to, between

several interpretations (in the sense of reading that is also that of music and theater): the voice does not betray a text. If it did, it would be in the sense that betrayal is a revelation: for example, the restless polylogue that divides up each atom of writing. Manifestation of the impossible truth on which it will have been necessary, at every instant, and despite repetitions, to decide once and for all. The utterance thus betrays, it unveils what will have, one day, carried it away, between the divisions of all the voices or those into which the same voice divides itself.

Facing the polylogue, on the lefthand page, citations from other texts (*Dissemination, Glas, The Postcard*[1]) that all say something about the cinder, mingle their ashes and the word "cendre" with something else. The citations co-appear along with it, they are "summoned" [*comparaissent*]: an incomplete archive, still burning or already consumed, recalling certain textual sites, the continuous, tormenting, obsessive meditation about what are and are not, what is meant – or silenced by, cinders. These citations are preceded by the word *animadversio*, which in Latin means "observation," "perception," or "call to attention," and which I chose in homage to the journal *Anima*.

1. Although it is not cited, another text is alluded to (p. 75): "Télépathie," a kind of supplement to *The Postcard*, which, like *Glas*, is woven around the letters LAC, CLA, ALC, CAL, ACL, etc. (*Furor* 2 [1981] and *Confrontation* 10 [1983]). *Schibboleth* (1986), also dedicated to cinders, was not yet published.

prétations (au sens de la lecture mais aussi du théâtre et de la musique), la voix ne trahit pas un texte. Si elle le faisait, ce serait au sens où la trahison révèle: par exemple le polylogue remuant qui divise chaque atome d'écriture. Manifestation de l'impossible vérité dont il aura fallu, à chaque instant, et malgré des répétitions, en une seule fois décider. L'énonciation alors dénonce, elle dévoile ce qui l'aura emporté, un jour, entre toutes les voix qui se partagent ou que se partage la même voix.

En face du polylogue, sur la page de gauche, des citations d'autres textes (*La dissémination, Glas, La carte postale*[1]) qui tous disent quelque chose de la cendre, mêlent leurs cendres et le mot ''cendre'' à autre chose. Ils accompagnent, ils comparaissent: archive incomplète, encore en train de brûler ou déjà consumée, rappelant certains lieux du texte, la méditation continue, harcelée, obsédée de ce que sont et ne sont pas, veulent dire – ou taire, des cendres. Ces citations sont précédées du mot *animadversio* qui signifie en latin *attention, observation, remarque, rappel,* et que j'ai choisi en hommage à la revue *Anima*.

1. Bien qu'il ne soit pas cité, un autre texte est visé par une allusion (p. 75): *Télépathie,* sorte de supplément à *La carte postale* qui, comme *Glas,* se trame autour des lettres LAC, CLA ALC CAL, ACL, etc. (*Furor* 2, 1981 et *Confrontation* 10, 1983). *Schibboleth* (1986), aussi dédié aux cendres, n'était pas encoré publié.

Qu'on me permette de souligner enfin deux difficultés parmi d'autres dans la scénographie sonore qui fut tentée d'autre part. Tout d'abord, il fallait *à la fois* marquer et effacer l'accent sur le à de là dans ''il y a là cendre'' et ailleurs. Faire les deux à la fois était impossible et si le mot ''accent'' dit quelque chose du chant, c'est l'expérience de la cendre et du chant qui cherche ici son nom.

Puis si la version enregistrée donne à entendre deux voix, dont l'une paraît masculine, l'autre féminine, cela ne réduit pas le polylogue à un duo, voire à un duel. Et en effet la mention ''une autre voix,'' qu'on entend parfois sans la lire, aura souvent la valeur d'une mise en garde. Elle signale que chacune des deux voix se prête à d'autres encore. Je le répète, elles sont en nombre indéterminé: celle du signataire des textes ne figure que l'une d'entre elles, et il n'est pas sûr qu'elle soit masculine. Ni l'autre femme.

Mais les mots ''une autre voix'' ne rappellent pas seulement la multiplicité des personnes, ils appellent, ils demandent une autre voix: ''une autre voix, encore, encore une autre voix.'' C'est un désir, un ordre, une prière ou une promesse, comme on voudra: ''une autre voix, que vienne à cette heure, encore, une autre voix. . . .'' Un ordre ou une promesse, le désir d'une prière, je ne sais pas, pas encore.

J.D.

May I emphasize finally two difficulties among others in the resonant scenography that was attempted elsewhere. To begin with, it was necessary at once to mark and efface the accent on the "à" in "là" in "il y a là cendre" and elsewhere. To do both at once was impossible and if the word "accent" says something about "song," it is the experience of cinders and song that here seeks its name.

So if the recorded version makes two voices heard, of which one seems masculine, the other feminine, that does not reduce the polylogue to a duet, much less to a duel. And the effect of mentioning "another voice," which one sometimes hears without reading it, will often be to put one on one's guard. It signals that each of the two voices yields to still others. I repeat, they are indeterminate in number: the voice of the signatory of the texts is the figure of only one among others, and it is not certain whether this figure is masculine; nor whether the other is a woman.

But the words "another voice" recall not only the complex multiplicity of people, they "call," they "ask for" another voice: "another voice, again, yet another voice." It is a desire, an order, a prayer or a promise, as you wish: "another voice, may it come soon now, again, another voice . . ." An order or a promise, the desire of a prayer, I don't know, not yet.

J. D.

Feu la cendre

Cinders

Animadversiones

I

"S'écartant d'elle-même, s'y formant toute, presque sans reste, l'écriture d'un seul trait renie et reconnaît la dette. Effondrement extrême de la signature, loin du centre, voire des secrets qui s'y partagent pour disperser jusqu'à leur cendre.

"Que la lettre soit forte en cette seule indirection, et de toujours pouvoir manquer l'arrive, je n'en prendrai pas prétexte pour m'absenter à la pontualité d'une dédicace: R. Gasché, J.-J. Goux, J.-C Lebensztejn, J.-H. Miller, d'autres, il y a là cendre, reconnaîtront, peut-être, ce qui intervient ici de leur lecture. Décembre 1971."

I

"Moving off of itself, forming itself wholly therein, almost without remainder, writing denies and recognizes its debt in a single dash. The utmost disintegration of the signature, far from the center, indeed from the secrets that are shared there, divided up so as to scatter even their ashes.

"Though the letter gains strength solely from this indirection, and granted that it can always not arrive at the other side, I will not use this as a pretext to absent myself from the punctuality of a dedication: R. Gasché, J. J. Goux, J. C. Lebensztejn, J. H. Miller, others, cinders there are [il y a là cendre], will recognize, perhaps, what their reading has contributed here. December 1971."

— Et près de la fin, au bas de la dernière page, c'est comme si tu signais de ces mots: "Il y a là cendre." Je lisais, relisais, c'était si simple et pourtant je comprenais que je n'y étais pas, la phrase se retirait sans m'attendre vers son secret.

— D'autant plus que ce mot, là, vous ne le donniez plus à entendre. A l'écouter seulement, les yeux fermés, j'aimais me rassurer en murmurant la cendre, confondant ce là, oui, avec le singulier féminin d'un article définissant. Il fallait déchiffrer sans perdre l'équilibre, entre l'œil et l'oreille, je ne suis pas sûre d'avoir pu m'y arrêter.

— J'avais d'abord imaginé pour ma part que cendre était là, non pas ici mais là comme l'histoire à raconter: la cendre, ce vieux mot gris, ce thème poussiéreux de l'humanité, l'image immémoriale s'était d'elle-même décomposée, métaphore ou métonymie de soi, tel est le destin de toute cendre, séparée, consumée comme une cendre de cendre. Qui oserait encore se risquer au poème de la cendre? Le mot de cendre, on rêverait qu'il fût: lui-même une cendre en ce sens, là, là-bas, éloigné dans le passé, mémoire perdue pour ce qui n'est plus d'ici. Et par là, sa phrase aurait voulu dire, sans rien garder: la cendre n'est plus ici. Y fut-elle jamais?

— And near the end, at the bottom of the last page, it was as though you had signed with these words: "Cinders there are." I read, reread them; it was so simple, and yet I knew that I was not there; without waiting for me the phrase withdrew into its secret.

— All the more because this word, *là*, "there," you would no longer let it be heard. Listening only to it, with eyes closed, I liked putting my mind at rest by whispering "the cinder," confusing this *là*, "there," yes, with *la*, the singular feminine definite article. It was necessary to decipher without losing equilibrium between the eye and the ear; I am not sure that I was ever able to achieve it.

— As for me, I had at first imagined that cinders were there, not here but there, as a story to be told: cinder, this old gray word, this dusty theme of humanity, the immemorial image had decomposed from within, a metaphor or metonymy of itself, such is the destiny of every cinder, separated, consumed like a cinder of cinders. Who would still dare run the risk of a poem of the cinder? One might dream that the word "cinder" was itself a cinder in that sense, "there," "over there," in the distant past, a lost memory of what is no longer here. And thereby *[par là]* its phrase would have meant, without holding anything back: the cinder is no longer here. Was *[fut]* it ever?

33 . . .

– Il y a là cendre, quand cela fut, il y a près de dix ans, la phrase éloignait d'elle-même. En elle, elle portait le lointain. Malgré sa place et l'apparence elle ne se laissait pas signer, elle n'appartenait plus, un peu comme si, ne signifiant rien qui fût intelligible, elle venait de très loin à la rencontre de son présumé signataire qui ne la lisait même pas, la recevait à peine, la rêvait plutôt comme une légende, une fumée de tabac: ces mots qui sortent de votre bouche et vont se perdre sans reconnaissance.

– Suppose, voilà ce que j'aurais aimé lui demander (mais à qui? pour la première fois ce matin, dix ans après, je prends conscience jusqu'à pouvoir me l'avouer de ce qui à la lecture s'imprime en moi, au centre défendu mais préparé pour la jouissance muette: l'article absent devant telle cendre, en un mot la ressemblance esquissée par cet homophone là faisait trembler d'une femme le fantôme au fond du mot, dans la fumée, le nom propre au fond du nom commun. La cendre n'est pas ici mais il y a là Cendre.

– Qui est Cendre? Où est-elle? Où court-elle à cette heure? Si l'homophonie retient le nom singulier dans le nom commun, ce fut bien là, une personne disparue mais une chose qui en garde et à la fois perd la trace, la

– Cinders there are; when that happened *[fut]* nearly ten years ago the phrase withdrew from itself. The phrase carried distance within itself, within herself. Despite its venue and despite all appearances, it did not permit itself, did not permit herself, to sign; it no longer belonged; somewhat as if, signifying nothing that was *[fût]* intelligible, the phrase came from very far away to meet its supposed signatory, who did not even read it, who scarcely received it, dreamed it rather, like a legend or a saying, a whiff of tobacco smoke: these words that leave your mouth only to be lost in unrecognizability.

– Just suppose, this is what I would have liked to ask (but whom? This morning, for the first time, ten years later, I became aware to the point of being able to admit to myself that something about this reading is imprinted in me, in a place sheltered but ready for silent ecstasy: the article missing before such cinders, in a word, the resemblance sketched by this homophonic *là,* "there," made a feminine phantom tremble deep within the word, in the smoke, the proper name deep within the common noun. The cinder is not here, but Cinder there is.

– Who is Cinder? Where is she? Where did she run off to at this hour? If the homophony withholds the singular name within the common noun, it was surely "there," *là*; someone vanished but something preserved her trace and at the same time lost it, the

cendre. C'est là la cendre: ce qui garde pour ne plus même garder, vouant le reste à la dissipation, et ce n'est plus personne disparue laissant là cendre, seulement son nom mais illisible. Et rien n'interdit de penser que ce soit aussi le surnom du soi-disant signataire. Il y a là cendre, une phrase dit ainsi ce qu'elle fait, ce qu'elle est. Elle s'incinère à la seconde, sous vos yeux: mission impossible (mais je n'aime pas ce verbe, incinérer, je ne lui trouve aucune affinité avec la tendresse vulnérable, avec la patience d'une cendre. Il est actif, aigu, incisif).

– Non, la phrase ne dit pas ce qu'elle est, mais ce qu'elle *fut,* et comme ce vocable fut employé par vous déjà tant de fois depuis tout à l'heure, n'oubliez pas qu'il reste en mémoire de feu, du mot feu dans l'expression feu un tel ou feu une telle. Cendre de toutes nos étymologies perdues, *fatum, fuit, functus, defunctus.*

– La phrase dit ce qu'elle aura été, dès lors se donnant à elle-même, se donnant comme son propre nom, l'art consumé du secret: de l'exhibition savoir se garder.

– Suppose, aurais je demandé, que cette légende seulement signale, et pour ne rien dire d'autre que soi: je suis un signal de cendre, je rappelle quelque chose ou quel-

cinder. There the cinder is: that which preserves in order no longer to preserve, dooming the remnant to dissolution. And it is no longer the one who has disappeared who leaves cinders "there"; it is only her still unreadable name. And nothing prevents us from thinking that this may also be the nickname of the so-called signatory. Cinders there are, the phrase thus says what it does, what it is. It immediately incinerates itself, in front of your eyes: an impossible mission (but I do not like this verb, "to incinerate"; I find in it no affinity with the vulnerable tenderness, with the patience of a cinder. The verb is active, acute, incisive).

– No, the phrase does not say what it is, but what it was *[fut],* and since this vocable was *[fut]* just used by you so many times, do not forget that it remains in memory of the departed *[feu],* of the word *feu* in the idiom, "the late so and so," the departed, the bereaved. Cinder of all our lost etymologies, *fatum, fuit, functus, defunctus.*

– The sentence says what it will have been, from the moment it gives itself up to itself, giving itself as its own proper name, the consumed (and consummate) art of the secret: of knowing how to keep itself from showing.

– Just suppose, I would have asked, that this saying only gives a signal and only in order to say nothing other than itself: I am a cinder signal, I recall something or someone of whom I will say nothing but

qu'un dont je ne dirai rien mais ce tracé visiblement pour ne rien dire aura dû annuler le dit de son dire, le donner au feu, le détruire dans la flamme et non autrement. Pas de cendre sans feu.

Cela se doit au feu et pourtant, si possible, sans l'ombre d'un sacrifice, à midi, sans dette, sans Phénix et l'unique phrase vient à placer, au lieu d'aucun placement, le lieu seulement d'une incinération. Elle n'avoue que l'incinération en cours dont elle reste le monument, tacite à peu près, ce peut être là –

– Mais pourquoi auriez-vous donné au feu? Pour garder, caché, ou pour perdre en laissant voir le gris du deuil, le demi-deuil qui ne tient à soi que le temps d'une cendre? Pourquoi là cendre? Lieu de brûlure mais de quoi, de qui? Tant qu'on ne le sait pas, et vous ne le saurez jamais, déclare la phrase en ce qu'elle dit de plus haut, l'incinéré n'est plus rien fors la cendre, un reste qui se doit de ne plus rester, ce lieu de rien qui soit, un lieu pur se chiffrât-il.

– Pur est le mot. Il appelle un feu. Il y a là cendre, voilà qui prend place en laissant place, pour donner à entendre: rien n'aura eu lieu que le lieu. Il y a là cendre: il y a lieu.

this rough sketch obviously in order to say that nothing will have had to annul what is said in its saying, to give it to the fire, to destroy it in the flame, and not otherwise. No cinder without fire *[feu]*.

That is what is owed to the fire, and yet, if possible, without the shadow of a sacrifice, at noon, without debt, without the Phoenix, thus the unique phrase comes to set into place, in the place of no emplacement, the place solely of an incineration. The sentence avows only the ongoing incineration, of which it remains the almost silent monument: this can be "there," *là* –

– But why would you have given it to the fire? To preserve the hiddenness of mourning's ashen grayness, or to undo it by letting it be seen, the half-mourning that persists only as long as the time of a cinder? Why cinders "there"? The place of burning, but of what, of whom? As long as one does not know, and you will never know, the sentence says what it said earlier, the incinerated is no longer nothing, nothing but the cinder, the innermost cinder furnace, a remnant that must no longer remain, this place of nothing that may be, a pure place was marked out.

– Pure is the word. It calls for fire. Cinders there are, this is what takes place in letting a place occur, so that it will be understood: Nothing will have taken place but the place. Cinders there are: Place there is (*il y a lieu*).

39 . . .

– Où? Ici? Là? Où sont des mots sur une page?

– Il y a prescription. L'idiome "il y a lieu," jamais vous ne le traduirez, non plus qu'un nom propre caché or le voici qui déporte tout: vers la reconnaissance, la dette, le devoir, la prescription. Il y a lieu de ceci, un nom propre, il y a lieu de faire ceci ou cela, de donner, de rendre, de célébrer, d'aimer. Et de fait le paysage de la légende (il y a là cendre) l'entoure d'amitié, la grâce rendue tout de même que la dissémination. Il y a là cendre, cela fut, en somme, comme le titre fragile et friable du livre. Discrètement écartée, la dissémination phrase ainsi en cinq mots ce qui par le feu se destine à la dispersion sans retour, la pyrification de qui ne reste pas et ne revient à personne.

– Si un lieu même s'encercle de feu (tombe en cendre finalement, tombe en tant que nom), il n'est plus. Reste la cendre. Il y a là cendre, traduis, la cendre n'est pas, elle n'est pas ce qui est. Elle reste de ce qui n'est pas, pour ne rappeler au fond friable d'elle que non-être ou imprésence. L'être sans présence n'a pas été et ne sera pas plus là où il y a la cendre et parlerait cette autre mémoire. Là, où cendre veut dire la différence entre ce qui reste et ce qui est, y arrive-t-elle, là?

– Where? Here? There? Where are the words on a page?

– There are prescribed limits. The idiom *il y a lieu,* you will never translate it, no more than you will a hidden proper name, for this is what carries everything away: toward the recognition, the debt, the obligation, the prescribed limit. There is a place for this, a proper name, place there is for doing this or that, for giving, rendering, celebrating, loving. And because of this, the locality of the legend ("cinders there are") surrounds it with friendship, bestowing grace and dissemination at the same time. Cinders there are, that was *[fut]* finally like the fragile, singed, and crumbling title of the book, *Dissemination.* Discreetly pushed to the side, dissemination thus expresses in five words *[il y a là cendre]* what is destined, by the fire, to dispersion without return, the pyrification of what does not remain and returns to no one.

– If a place is itself surrounded by fire (falls finally to ash, into a cinder tomb), it no longer is. Cinder remains, cinder there is, which we can translate: the cinder is not, is not what is. It remains *from* what is not, in order to recall at the delicate, charred bottom of itself only non-being or non-presence. Being without presence has not been and will no longer be there where there is cinder and where this other memory would speak. There, where cinder means the difference between what remains and what is, will she ever reach it, there?

40 . . .

-Il trouve peut-être indécent d'avoir à commenter, à lire même et à citer cette phrase: c'est proprement encenser, pour dire le mot. Quoi qu'il prétende, ''il y a là cendre'' reste à lui. Et tout ce que nous en dirons et multiplierons ici, de la signature légale qu'il feint de détériorer il le reliera, il nous le reprendra, le donnera au foyer de son propre incendie – ou de sa propre famille: il n'y a cendre que selon l'âtre, le foyer, quelque feu ou lieu. La cendre comme maison de l'être . . .

-Ta précaution est ingénue. Il répondra ce qu'il voudra, la phrase a beau paraître dans un livre portant sa signature, elle ne lui appartient pas, il avoue l'avoir lue avant de l'écrire. Elle, cette cendre, lui fut donnée ou prêtée par tant d'autres, par tant d'oublis et d'ailleurs personne ici ne l'encense d'un commentaire, ce secret. Nous n'en dévoilons littéralement rien, rien qui au bout du compte ne la laisse intacte, vierge (il n'aime que ça), indéchiffrable, impassiblement tacite, bref à l'abri de la cendre qu'il y a et qui est elle. Car abandonnée à sa solitude, témoin de qui ou de quoi, la phrase ne dit même pas la cendre. Cette chose dont on ne sait rien, ni quel passé porte encore cette poussière grise de mots, ni quelle substance vint s'y consumer avant de s'y éteindre (savez-vous

41 . . .

— Perhaps he finds it unseemly to have to comment, even to read and to cite this phrase: he is, in effect, "really incensed" at having, in a word, "to incense" it. Regardless what he may say, "cinder there is" remains his. And everything we will say and advance here about it, concerning the legal signature that he pretends to undermine, he will reinstate it, he will take it back again, will give it to the hearth of its own burning — or of its own family. There are cinders only insofar as there is the hearth, the fireplace, some fire or place. Cinder as the house of being . . .

— Your precaution is naive. He will answer however he chooses. While the phrase appears in a book bearing his signature, it does not belong to him. He admits having already read it before writing it, before writing her. She, this cinder, was given or lent to him by so many others, through so much forgetting, and besides, no one here flatters this secret with a commentary. We literally unveil nothing of her, nothing that in the final account does not leave her intact, virginal (that's the only thing he loves), undecipherable, impassively tacit, in a word, sheltered from the cinder that there is and that she is. For abandoned to its solitude, witness to whomever or whatever, the sentence does not even say the cinder. This thing of which one knows nothing, knows neither what past is still carried in these gray dusty words, nor what substance came to consume itself there before extinguishing itself there (do you know

II

"Pure and figureless, this light burns all. It burns itself in the all-burning [le brule-tout] it is, leaves, of itself or anything, no trace, no mark, no sign of passage. Pure consuming destruction, pure effusion of light without shadow, noon without contrary, without resistance, without obstacle, waves, showers, streams ablaze with light: '[. . .] (Lichtgüsse) [. . .].' "

"The all-burning is 'an essenceless by-play, pure accessory of the substance that rises without ever setting (ein wesenloses Beiherspielen an dieser Substanz die nur aufgeht, ohne in sich niederzugehen), without becoming a subject, and without consolidating through the self (Selbst) its differences.' "

II

"Pure et sans figure, cette lumière brûle tout. Elle se brûle dans le brûle-tout qu'elle est, ne laisse d'elle-même ni de rien, aucune trace, aucune marque, aucun signe de passage. Pure consumation, pure effusion de lumière sans ombre, midi sans contraire, sans résistance, sans obstacle; onde, ondées, flots enflammés de lumière: "[. . .] (Lichtgüsse) [. . .]."

"Le brûle-tout est 'un jeu sans essence, pur accessoire de la substance qui se lève sans jamais se coucher (ein wesenloses Beiherspielen an dieser Substanz die nur aufgeht, ohne in sich niederzugehen) sans devenir sujet et sans stabiliser ses différences par le moyen du soi-même (Selbst)'."

combien de types de cendres distinguent les natura-
listes? et de quel ''bois'' telles cendres parfois rappellent un désir?), une telle chose, dira-t-on encore qu'elle
garde même une identité de cendre? Au présent, ici
maintenant, voilà une matière – visible mais lisible à
peine – qui ne renvoyant qu'à elle-même ne fait plus
trace, à moins qu'elle ne trace qu'en perdant la trace
qu'elle reste à peine

– qu'elle reste pour peu

– mais c'est justement ce qu'il appelle la trace, cet effa-
cement. J'ai maintenant l'impression que le meilleur
paradigme de la trace, pour lui, ce n'est pas, comme certains l'ont cru, et lui aussi peut-être, la piste de chasse,
le frayage, le sillon dans le sable, le sillage dans la mer,
l'amour du pas pour son empreinte, mais la cendre (ce
qui reste sans rester de l'holocauste, du brûle-tout, de
l'incendie l'encens)

– Qu'elle reste pour très peu de personnes, et pour peu
qu'on y touche elle tombe, elle ne tombe pas en cendres,
elle se perd, et jusqu'à la cendre de ses cendres. En écrivant ainsi, il brûle une fois de plus, il brûle ce qu'il adore
encore mais qu'il a déjà brûlé, il s'y acharne

how many types of cinders the naturalists distinguish? and for what "wood" such cinders sometimes
recall a desire?); will one still say of such a thing that
it even preserves the identity of a cinder? At present,
here and now, there is something material – visible
but scarcely readable – that, referring only to itself,
no longer makes a trace, unless it traces only by
losing the trace it scarcely leaves

– that it just barely remains

– but that is just what he calls the trace, this efface-
ment. I have the impression now that the best paradigm for the trace, for him, is not, as some have believed, and he as well, perhaps, the trail of the hunt,
the fraying, the furrow in the sand, the wake in the
sea, the love of the step for its imprint, but the cinder
(what remains without remaining from the holocaust, from the all-burning, from the incineration
the incense)

– That it remains for very few people, and, however
slightly one touches it, it falls, it does not fall into
cinders, it gets lost down to the cinder of its cinders.
In writing this way, he burns one more time, he
burns what he still adores although he has already
burned it, he is intent on it

". . . feu artiste. Le mot lui-même (Beiherspielen) *joue l'exemple* (Beispiel) *à côté de l'essence."*

"Le brûle-tout – qui n'a lieu qu'une fois et se répète cependant à l'infini – s'écarte si bien de toute généralité essentielle qu'il ressemble à la pure différence d'un accident absolu. Jeu et pure différence, voilà le secret d'un brûle tout imperceptible, le torrent de feu qui s'embrase lui-même. S'emportant elle-même, la différence pure est différente d'elle-même, donc indifférente. Le jeu pur de la différence n'est rien, il ne se rapporte même pas à son propre incendie. La lumière s'enténèbre avant même de devenir sujet."

"Comment de cette consumation sans limite peut-il rester quelque chose qui amorce le procès dialectique et ouvre l'histoire?"

"Comment le pur du pur, le pire du pire, l'incendie panique du brûle-tout pousserait-il quelque monument, fût il crématoire? quelque forme géométrique, solide, par exemple une pyramis *qui garde trace de la mort? Pyramis, c'est aussi un gâteau de miel et de farine. On l'offrait en récompense d'une nuit blanche à qui restait ainsi éveillé."*

"S'il détruit jusqu'à sa lettre et son corps, comment le brûle-tout peut-il garder trace de lui-même et entamer une histoire où il se conserve en se perdant?

Ici s'éprouve la force implacable du sens, de la médiation, du laborieux négatif. Pour être ce qu'il est, pureté du jeu, de la différence, de la consumation, le brûle-tout doit passer dans son contraire: se garder, garder son mouvement de perte, apparaître comme ce qu'il est dans sa disparition même. Dès qu'il apparaît, dès que le feu se montre, il reste, il se retient, il se perd comme feu. La pure différence, différente de soi, cesse d'être ce qu'elle est pour rester ce qu'elle est. C'est l'origine de l'histoire, le commencement du déclin, le

". . . fire artist. The word itself (Beiherspielen) plays the example (Beispiel) beside the essence."

"The all-burning – that has taken place once and nonetheless repeats itself ad infinitum – diverges so well from all essential generality that it resembles the pure difference of an absolute accident. Play and pure difference, those are the secret of an imperceptible all-burning, the torrent of fire that sets itself ablaze. Letting itself get carried away, pure difference is different from itself, therefore indifferent. The pure play of difference is nothing, does not even relate to its own conflagration. The light envelops itself in darkness even before becoming subject."

"How, from this consuming destruction without limit, can there remain something that primes the dialectical process and opens history?"

"How would the purest of the pure, the worst of the worst, the panic blaze of the all-burning, put forth some monument, even were it a crematory? Some stable, geometric, solid form, for example, a pyramis that guards the trace of death? Pyramis is also a cake of honey and flour. It was offered as a reward for a sleepless night to the one who thus remained awake."

"If the all-burning destroys up to its letter and its body, how can it guard the trace of itself and breach/broach a history where it preserves itself in losing itself?"

Here is experienced the implacable force of sense, of mediation, of the hard-working negative. In order to be what it is, purity of play, of difference, of consuming destruction, the all-burning must pass into its contrary, guard itself, guard its own monument of loss, appear as what it is in its very disappearance. As soon as it appears, as soon as the fire shows itself, it remains, it keeps hold of itself, it loses itself as fire. Pure difference, different from (it)self, ceases to be what it is in order to remain what it is. That is the origin of history, the beginning of the going down [déclin], the set-

45 . . .

coucher du soleil, le passage à la subjectivité occiden-
tale. Le feu devient pour-soi et c'est perdu; encore pire
puisque meillieur.

Alors au lieu de tout brûler on commence à aimer les
fleurs. La religion des fleurs suit la religion du soleil.
L'érection de la pyramide garde la vie – le mort – pour
donner lieu au pour-soi de l'adoration. Elle a la signifi-
cation d'un sacrifice, d'une offre par laquelle le brûle-
tout s'annule, ouvre l'anneau, le resserre dans l'anni-
versaire de la révolution solaire en se sacrifiant
comme brûle-tout donc en se gardant.''
''Chance de la substance, de la restance déterminée en
subsistance.''

''La différence et le jeu de la lumière pure, la dissémma-
tion panique et pyromane, le brûle-tout s'offre en ho-
locauste au pour-soi, gibt sich dem Fürsichsein zum
Opfer. Il se sacrifie mais c'est pour rester, assurer sa
garde, se lier à lui-même, strictement, devenir lui-
même, pour-soi, auprès de soi. Pour se sacrifier, il se
brûle.''

''Inversion panique, sans limite: le mot holocauste *qui*
se trouve traduire Opfer *est plus approprié au texte que*
le mot de Hegel lui-même. Dans ce sacrifice, tout (ho-
los) est brûlé (caustos) et le feu ne pourra s'éteindre
qu'attisé.''

''Qu'este-ce qui se met en jeu dans cet holocauste du
jeu lui-même?

Ceci peut-être: le don, le sacrifice, la mise en jeu ou à
feu de tout, l'holocauste, sont en puissance d'ontolo-
gie. Sans l'holocauste le mouvement dialectique et
l'histoire de l'être ne pouvaient pas s'ouvrir, s'engager
dans l'anneau de leur anniversaire, s'annuler en pro-
duisant la course solaire d'Orient en Occident. Avant,
si l'on pouvait compter ici avec le temps, avant toute
chose, avant tout étant déterminable, il y a, il y avait, il y

ting of the sun, the passage to occidental subjectivity. Fire becomes for-(it)self and is lost; yet worse [pire] since better.

Then in place of burning all, one begins to love flowers. The religion of flowers follows the religion of the sun.

The erection of the pyramid guards life – the dead – in order to
give rise [donner lieu] to the for-(it)self of adoration. This has
the signification of a sacrifice, of an offer by which the all-burning
annuls itself, opens the annulus, contracts the annulus into the
anniversary of the solar revolution in sacrificing itself as the all-
burning, therefore in guarding itself."

"The chance of substance, of the remnance [restance] determined
as subsistence."

"The difference and the play of the pure light, the panic and pyromaniac dissemination, the all-burning offers itself as a holocaust to the for-(it)self, gibt sich dem Fürsichsein zum Opfer.
It sacrifices itself, but only to remain, to insure its guarding, to
bind itself to itself strictly, to become itself, for-(it)self, (close)-
by-(it)self. In order to sacrifice itself, it burns itself."

"A panic, limitless inversion: the word holocaust that happens to
translate Opfer is more appropriate to the text than the word of
Hegel himself. In this sacrifice, all (holos) is burned (caustos),
and the fire can go out only stoked."

"What puts itself in play in this holocaust of play itself?"

This perhaps: the gift, the sacrifice, the putting into play or the
setting on fire of everything, the holocaust contains the seeds of
ontology. Without the holocaust the dialectical movement and
the history of Being could not open themselves, engage themselves in the annulus of their anniversary, could not annul themselves in producing the solar course from Orient to Occident. Before, if one could count here with time, before everything, before
every determinable being [étant], there is, there was, there will

47 . . .

aura eu l'événement irruptif du don. Événement qui n'a plus aucun rapport avec ce qu'on désigne couramment sous ce mot. On ne peut donc plus penser la donation à partir de l'être, mais 'le contraire' pourrait-on dire si cette inversion logique était ici pertinente au moment où il ne s'agit pas encore de logique mais de l'origine de la logique. Dans Zeit und Sein, *le don du* es gibt *se donne à penser avant le* Sein *dans le* es gibt Sein *et déplace tout ce qu'on détermine sous le nom d'*Ereignis, *mot souvent traduit par* événement." [. . .]

"*. . . le procès du don (avant l'échange), procès qui n'est pas un procès mais un holocauste, un holocauste de l'holocauste,* engage *l'histoire de l'être mais ne lui appartient pas. Le don* n'est pas, *l'holocauste* n'est pas, *si du moins* il y en a. *Mais dès qu'il brûle (l'incendie n'est pas un étant) il doit, se brûlant lui-même, brûler son opération de brûler et commencer à être. Cette réflexion, ce reflet de l'holocauste engage l'histoire, la dialectique du sens, l'ontologie, le spéculatif. Le spéculatif est le reflet* (speculum) *de l'holocauste de l'holocauste, l'incendie réfléchi et rafraîchi par la glace du miroir*". [. . .]

"*Il y a là un fatum du don, et cette nécessité se disait dans le 'doit'* (muss) *qui nous l'indiquait plus haut [. . .]. Je te donne – don pur, sans échange, sans retour – mais que je le veuille ou non, le don se garde et dès lors tu dois. Pour que le don se garde, tu dois. [. . .] Le don ne peut être qu'un sacrifice, tel est l'axiome de la raison spéculative. Même s'il surgit 'avant' la philosophie et la religion, le don a pour destination ou détermination, pour* Bestimmung, *un retour à soi dans la philosophie, vérité de la religion.*"

have been the irruptive event of the gift [don]. *An event that no more has any relation with what is currently designated under this word. Thus giving can no longer be thought starting from Being* [être], *but 'the contrary,' it could be said, if this logical inversion here were pertinent when the question is not yet logic but the origin of logic. In* Zeit und Sein, *the gift of the* es gibt *gives itself to be thought before the* Sein *in the* es gibt Sein *and displaces all that is determined under the name* Ereignis, *a word translated by event.*" [. . .]

"*. . . the process of the gift (before exchange), the process that is not a process but a holocaust, a holocaust of the holocaust, engages the history of Being but does not belong to it. The gift is not; the holocaust is not; if at least something there is* [il y en a]. *But as soon as it burns (the blaze is not a being) it must, burning itself, burn its very act of burning and begin to be. This reflection (in both senses of the word) of the holocaust engages history, the dialectic of sense, ontology, the speculative. The speculative is the reflection (speculum) of the holocaust's holocaust, the blaze reflected and cooled by the glass, the ice, of the mirror.*" [. . .]

"*A fatum of the gift there is* [Il y a là], *and this necessity was said in the 'must'* (muss, doit) *we indicated above [. . .]. I give you – a pure gift, without exchange, without return – but whether I want this or not, the gift guards itself, keeps itself, and from then on you must-owe,* tu dois. [. . .] *The gift can only be a sacrifice, that is the axiom of speculative reason. Even if it upsurges 'before' philosophy and religion, the gift has for its destination or determination, for its* Bestimmung, *a return to self in philosophy, religion's truth.*"

49 . . .

et je le sens,
je veux dire l'odeur du corps, peut-être du sien. Toutes
ces cendres, il s'acharne en elles.

— On dit ''cendres chaudes,'' ''cendres froides,'' selon
que le feu s'y souvient encore, y couve ou ne fomente
plus. Mais là? Quand la cendre toute en phrase n'a pour
consistance que sa syntaxe et de corps qu'en son voca-
bulaire? Les mots, ça fait chaud ou froid? Ni chaud ni
froid. Et la forme grise de ces lettres? Entre le blanc et le
noir, la couleur de l'écriture ressemble à la seule ''litté-
ralité'' de la cendre qui tienne encore dans un langage.
Dans une cendre de mots, dans la cendre d'un nom, la
cendre elle-même, la littérale – celle qu'il aime – a disparu. Le nom de cendre est une cendre encore de la cendre même.

— C'est pourquoi la cendre dans une sentence ici n'est
plus, mais il y a là cendre.

— Là, une incinération de l'article défini laisse en cendres la cendre même. Il la disperse et la garde par là, elle,
à la seconde.

— Lui (mais c'est peut-être elle, la cendre), peut-être
sait-il ce qu'il voulait ainsi incendier, célébrer, encen-

and I sense it, I mean the
odor of the body, perhaps his. All these cinders, he
feels them burning in his flesh.

— One says "warm cinders," "cold cinders," depend-
ing whether the fire still lingers there or no longer
stirs. But there? Where the cinder within a sentence
has for consistency only its syntax and for body only
its vocabulary? Does this make the words warm or
cold? Neither warm nor cold. And the gray form of
these letters? Between black and white, the color of
writing resembles the only "literality" of the cinder
that still inheres in a language. In a cinder of words,
in the cinder of a name, the cinder itself, the literal –
that which he loves – has disappeared. The name
"cinder" is still a cinder of the cinder itself.

— That is why the cinder in a sentence here no longer
is, but cinder there is.

— There, *là,* an incineration of the definite article
leaves the cinder itself in cinders. It disperses it and
thereby *[par là]* preserves it, preserves her, in an instant.

— He (but perhaps it is she, *la* cinder) perhaps he
knows what he thus wished to set on fire, to cele-
brate, to ignite with praise in the secret of the sen-

ser dans le secret de la sentence, peut-être le savent-ils encore, peut-être en sait-il du moins quelque chose. Mais cette nuit même il peut encore découvrir de l'inconnu ou de l'inconscient à cette légende qu'il dit tantôt avoir lue tantôt avoir, je me rappelle son mot, forgée. Il l'avait prononcé avec un accent anglais, ma "forgerie de contrefacteur." Or il va bien mourir. Et si peu de temps que ce soit, la petite phrase a quelque chance de lui survivre, plus cendre que jamais, là, et moins que jamais sans personne à dire moi.

— Mais le contrefacteur peut mentir, il ment j'en suis presque sûre, comme d'expérience, il n'y a sans doute aucun vrai secret au fond de cette phrase, aucun nom propre déterminé. Un jour il m'a confié mais je ne le crois jamais que la première lettre à peu près de chaque mot I.L.Y.A.L.C. était l'initiale d'un autre mot, le tout proférant, mais dans une langue étrangère, une toute autre déclaration, et que cette dernière aurait joué le rôle d'un nom propre codé, en vérité sa signature chiffrée. Je n'en ai rien cru, il venait d'inventer la supercherie, il peut toujours mentir ou ne pas même être assuré de ce qu'il dit savoir. C'est précisément à ce point qu'il y a la cendre. S'il était sûr en vérité de son savoir, pourquoi aurait-il eu ce désir d'écrire et surtout de publier une

tence, perhaps they still know it, perhaps he knows at least something about it. But even tonight he may still discover what is unknown or unconscious in this saying that he sometimes says he has read and sometimes, I recall his expression, forged. He had pronounced it with an English accent, my "counterfeiter's forgery." He will of course die someday; and for however brief a time, the little phrase has some chance of surviving him, more a cinder than ever, there, and less than ever without anyone to say "I."

— But the counterfeiter can lie, he's lying, I am almost sure of it, from experience. There is doubtless no real secret at the bottom of this sentence, no determined proper name. Once he confided to me, but I still do not believe that the first letter of almost every word, I.L.Y.A.L.C. *[il y a là cendre]*, was the first letter of another word, all of it expressing, but in a foreign language, an entirely different statement, which would have played the role of a coded proper name, in truth his ciphered signature. I believed none of it, he had just invented the hoax, he can always lie or not even be certain of what he claims to know. It is precisely at this point that the cinder is there. If he were sure of the truth of his knowledge, why would he have this desire to write and above all to publish a phrase that makes itself indeterminate in

phrase qui s'indétermine ainsi? Pourquoi mettre en dérive et clandestiner de la sorte une proposition aussi lisible? Sa proposition, qu'il y ait là cendre, voilà qu'elle consiste, dans son extrême fragilité comme dans le peu de temps dont elle dispose (sa vie aura été si courte) en ce non-savoir vers lequel se précipitent, toujours de pair, l'écriture et l'aveu. L'un l'autre, l'une l'autre dans la même crypte se compulsent.

– Par le retour patient, harcelant, ironique de l'exégèse qui n'avance à rien et que les ingénus trouveraient indécente, serions-nous en train de modeler l'urne d'un langage pour cette phrase de cendre qu'il a, lui, abandonnée à sa chance et au sort, une vertu d'autodestruction faisant feu toute seule en plein cœur?

– Mais l'urne de langage est si fragile. Elle s'effrite et tu souffles aussitôt dans une poussière de mots qui sont la cendre même. Et si tu la confies au papier c'est pour mieux t'enflammer mon enfant, tu te ravales aussitôt. Non, ce n'est pas le tombeau dont il aurait rêvé pour qu'un travail de deuil, comme ils disent, y ait lieu de prendre son temps. Dans cette phrase je vois: le tombeau d'un tombeau, le monument d'une tombe impossible – interdite, comme la mémoire d'un cénotaphe, la

this way? Why set adrift and "clandestine" in this way such a readable proposition? His proposition, that cinders there were, finally consists, in its extreme fragility and in the little time at its disposal (its life will have been so short), of this non-knowledge toward which writing and recognition, always a pair, are precipitated. One and the other, both of them, are compelled into the same crypt.

– Through the patient, tormenting, ironic return of the exegesis that leads to nothing and which the unsophisticated would find unseemly, would we be molding the urn of a language for this cinder sentence, which he, he, has abandoned to its chance and to fate, a self-destructive virtue firing on its own right into the heart.

– But the urn of language is so fragile. It crumbles and immediately you blow into the dust of words which are the cinder itself. And if you entrust it to paper, it is all the better to inflame you with, my dear, you will eat yourself up immediately. No, this is not the tomb he would have dreamed of in order that there may be a place *[y ait lieu]*, as they say, for the work of mourning to take its time. In this sentence I see the tomb of a tomb, the monument of an impossible tomb – forbidden, like the memory of a

patience refusée du deuil, refusée aussi la lente décomposition abritée, située, logée, hospitalisée en toi pendant que tu manges les morceaux (il n'a pas voulu manger le morceau mais il l'a dû). Une incinération célèbre peut-être le rien du tout, sa destruction sans retour mais folle de son désir et de sa ruse (pour mieux tout garder mon enfant), l'affirmation disséminale à corps perdu mais aussi tout le contraire, le non catégorique au labour du deuil, un non de feu. Comment accepter de travailler pour monseigneur le deuil?

– Comment ne pas l'accepter? Il est cela même, le deuil, l'histoire de son refus, le récit de ta révolution, ta rébellion, mon ange, quand elle entre en histoire et à minuit tu épouses un prince. Quant à l'urne de langue, fût-elle de feu, ne la crois pas si friable. Et ne mens pas, tu sais bien ce qu'une phrase est solide. Par sa disparition même elle résiste à tant et tant d'éclipses, elle garde toujours une chance de revenir, elle s'encense à l'infini, c'est beaucoup plus sûr au fond que le placement de l'archive dans un béton surarmé à destination de nos neveux extra-terrestres. La phrase se pare de toutes ses morts. Et si mieux tu te ravales, dit la grand-mère et le loup pour qui tu travailles, c'est encore au bénéfice du deuil.

cenotaph, deprived of the patience of mourning, denied also the slow decomposition that shelters, locates, lodges, hospitalizes itself in you while you eat the pieces (he did not want to eat the piece but was forced to). An incineration celebrates perhaps the nothing of the all, its destruction without return but mad with its desire and with its cunning (all the better to preserve everything, my dear), the desperately disseminal affirmation but also just the opposite, the categorical "no" to the laborious work of mourning, a "no" of fire. Can one ever accept working for His Highness Mourning?

– How can one not accept it? That is what mourning is, the history of its refusal, the narrative of your revolution, your rebellion, my angel, when it enters into history and at midnight you marry a prince. As for the urn of the spoken tongue, even were *[fût]* it a tongue of fire, do not think that it breaks up easily. And do not lie, you well know how solid a sentence is. By its very disappearance it resists so very many eclipses, it always has a chance of returning, it "incenses" itself to infinity. This is so much more certain finally than placing the archive in a reinforced beam destined for our extra-terrestrial cousins. The sentence is adorned with all of its dead. And all the better to eat yourself with, say the grandmother and the wolf for whom you work; it is still to the benefit of mourning.

III

"*. . . Et finir cette Deuxième Lettre: '. . . Réfléchis donc à cela et prends garde d'avoir à te repentir un jour de ce que tu laisserais aujourd'hui se divulguer indignement. La plus grande sauvegarde sera de ne pas écrire, mais d'apprendre par cœur . . . to mè graphein all'ekmanthanein . . . car il est impossible que les écrits ne finissent par tomber dans le domaine public. Aussi, au grand jamais, je n'ai moi-même écrit sur ces questions . . . oud'estin sungramma Platônos ouden oud'estai, il n'y a pas d'ouvrage de Platon et il n'y en aura pas. Ce qu'à présent l'on désigne sous ce nom Sôkratous estin kalou kai neou gegonotos . . . est de Socrate au temps de sa belle jeunesse. Adieu et obéis-moi. Aussitôt que tu auras lu et relu cette lettre, brûle-la . . .'*"

– *J'espère que celle-ci ne se perdra pas. Vite, un double . . . graphite . . . carbone . . . relu cette lettre . . . brûle-la. Il y a là cendre. Et maintenant il faudrait distinguer, entre deux répétitions . . .*

III

"*. . . And to finish that Second Letter: '. . . Consider these facts and take care lest you sometime come to repent of having now unwisely published your views. It is a very great safeguard to learn by heart instead of writing . . . to me graphein all'ekmanthanien. . . . It is impossible for what is written not to be disclosed. That is the reason why I have never written anything about these things . . . oud'estin sungramma Platonos ouden oud'estai, and why there is not and will not be any written work of Plato's own. What are now called his . . . Sokratous estin kalou kai neou gegonotos . . . are the work of a Socrates embellished and modernized. Farewell and believe. Read this letter now at once many times and burn it. . . .'*"

– *I hope this one won't get lost. Quick, a duplicate . . . graphite . . . carbon . . . reread this letter . . . burn it. Cinders there are [Il y a là cendre]. And now, to distinguish, between two repetitions . . .*

– Si c'était moi, j'aurais préféré n'avoir jamais écrit cela, je l'aurais aussitôt brûlé.

– Cela fut fait, non?

– Tu disais tout à l'heure qu'il ne pouvait pas y avoir de phrase d'''aujourd'hui'' pour ce mot de cendre. Si, il n'y en a qu'une peut-être dont la publication soit digne, elle dirait le brûle-tout, autrement dit holocauste et le four crématoire, en allemand dans toutes les langues juives du monde.

– Vous dites ne plus vous souvenir du lieu où la légende, une seconde fois, dans le même livre, comme un murmure de Platon pour occuper l'enceinte . . .

– Un murmure parfumé, le pharmakon désigne parfois une sorte d'encens, et l'itération, la seconde qu'elle est aussi ferait penser à une citation mais elle ne recommence qu'une première et une dernière fois à la fois. Si vous ne vous rappelez plus, c'est que l'incinération suit son cours et la consumation va de soi, la cendre même. Trace destinée, comme toute, à disparaître d'elle-même pour égarer la voie autant que pour rallumer une mémoire. La cendre est juste: parce que sans trace, justement elle trace plus qu'une autre, et comme l'autre trace.

– If it were I, I would have preferred never to have written that, I would have burnt it at once.

– Was [fut] that not done?

– You just said that he could not have an "up to date" phrase for this cinder word. Yes, there is perhaps only one worth publishing, it would tell of the all-burning, otherwise called holocaust and the crematory oven, in German in all the Jewish languages of the world.

– You say you no longer remember the place where the legend, a second time, in the same book, like Plato murmuring in the enclosure of the pharmacy . . .

– A perfumed murmur, the pharmakon sometimes designates a kind of incense, and the second iteration, which looks like a citation, which pretends to be a citation, but it only starts up all over again the first time and the last time at the same time. If you no longer recall it, it is because the incineration follows its course and the consummation proceeds from itself, the cinder itself. Trace destined, like everything, to disappear from itself, as much in order to lose the way as to rekindle a memory. The cinder is exact: because without a trace it precisely traces more than an other, and as the other trace(s). Although it comes

La nuit passe. Au matin, on entend des coups à la porte. Ils semblent venir du dehors, cette fois, les coups . . ."
Deux coups. . . quatre. . ."

IV

"J'espère que celle-ci ne se perdra pas. Vite, un double . . . graphite . . . carbone . . . relu cette lettre . . . brûle-la. Et maintenant il faudrait distinguer, entre deux répétitions . . .
La nuit passe. Au matin, on entend des coups à la porte. Ils semblent venir du dehors, cette fois, les coups . . .
Trois coups . . ."

V

"Le 27 août 1979. Tu viens d'appeler. Ah non, surtout pas Phénix (d'ailleurs c'est d'abord pour moi, dans ma langue fondamentale, la marque . . ."

The night passes. In the morning, knocks are heard at the door. They seem to be coming from outside, this time . . .
Two knocks . . . four . . ."

IV

"I hope this one won't get lost. Quick, a duplicate . . . graphite . . . carbon . . . reread this letter . . . burn it. And now, to distinguish two repetitions . . .
The night passes. In the morning, knocks are heard at the door. They seem to be coming from outside, this time . . .
Three knocks . . ."

V

"27 August 1979. You just called. Ah no, above all not Phoenix (which for me, moreover, is first of all, in my fundamental language, the mark . . ."

Bien qu'elle arrive plus tôt dans l'ordre du livre et la reliure des pages, elle y fut inscrite après la seconde: elle ne figurait pas dans la première édition du même texte. Entre les deux versions, où est la cendre de l'autre, ici ou là?

– Or par ce juste retour des cendres, et depuis longtemps je t'observe quand tu écris, ce qui revient de ta course essoufflée fait sa voie d'une longue piste cendrée. Tu as beau t'en défendre, tu n'es volume qu'à te couvrir de cendres, comme la tête en signe de deuil.

– Il y a la rebellion contre Phénix et aussi l'affirmation du feu sans lieu ni deuil.

– La phrase reste pour moi visible et avant même de la relire son image dans mon souvenir s'imprime à la plurielle, il y a là cendres. Version fautive à enterrer, comme font les Juifs quand le nom de Dieu un manuscrit le blesse. Cela, l's muet pour ne pouvoir s'entendre et ne rien changer à l'ouïe, ma mémoire le jouait, elle jouait avec le singulier homophone un jeu plus discriminant, plus rassurant, sans doute. Mais ce là désormais signifiait que l'innombrable couvait tout uniquement sous la cendre. Incubation du feu couché sous la poussière.

earlier in the book and in the order of the pages, it was *[fut]* inscribed there after the second iteration: it did not figure in the first version of the text. Between the two versions, where is the cinder of the other, here or there?

– Now, through this precise return of the cinders, and for a long time I have observed you when you write, what returns from the breathless race makes its way on a long cinder track. No matter how much you resist it, you have mass and volume only when covered with cinders, as one covers one's head with ashes in a sign of mourning.

– There is rebellion against the Phoenix and also the affirmation of the fire without place or mourning.

– The sentence remains visible for me and even before rereading it, its image in my memory is imprinted in the plural: cinders there are. A faulty version to be buried, as do the Jews when a manuscript has wounded the name of God. The "s," silent so that it cannot be heard and to change nothing in the hearing, my memory played with that; and with the singular homophone *[cendre]* it played a game more discriminating, more reassuring, no doubt. But this "there" from now on signified that the innumerable lurks beneath the cinder. Incubation of the fire lurking beneath the dust.

VI

"Quant aux Envois *eux-mêmes, je ne sais pas si la lecture en est soutenable. Vous pourriez les considérer, si le cœur vous en dit, comme les restes d'une correspondance récemment détruite. Par le feu ou par ce qui d'une figure en tient lieu, plus sûr de ne rien laisser hors d'atteinte pour ce que j'aime appeler langue de feu, pas même la cendre s'il y a là cendre.*
Fors- une chance.''

VII

"Car les envois totalement incinérés n'ont pu être indiqués d'aucune marque.''

VIII

"Si tu m'avais écouté, tu durais tout brûlé et rien ne serait arrivé. Je veux dire au contraire que quelque chose d'ineffaçable serait arrivé, au lieu de . . .''

IX

"Rien n'est arrivé parce que tu as voulu garder (et donc perdre), ce qui en effet formait le sens de l'ordre venu

VI

"As for the 'Envois' themselves, I do not know if reading them is bearable. You might consider them, if you really wish to, as the remainders of a recently destroyed correspondence. Destroyed by fire or by that which figuratively takes its place, more certain of leaving nothing out of the reach of what I like to call the tongue of fire, not even the cinders if cinders there are [s'il y a là cendre]. Save [fors] a chance."

VII

"For the totally incinerated envois could not be indicated by any mark."

VIII

"If you had listened to me, you would have burned everything, and nothing would have arrived. I mean on the contrary that something ineffaceable would have arrived, in the place of . . ."

IX

"Nothing has arrived because you wanted to preserve (and therefore to lose), which in effect formed the sense of the order coming

– Le feu: ce qu'on ne peut pas éteindre dans cette trace parmi d'autres qu'est une cendre. Mémoire ou l'oubli, comme tu voudras, mais du feu, trait qui rapporte encore à de la brûlure. Sans doute le feu s'est-il retiré, l'incendie maîtrisé, mais s'il y a là cendre, c'est que du feu reste en retrait. Par sa retraite encore il feint d'avoir abandonné le terrain. Il camoufle encore, il se déguise, sous la multiplicité, la poussière, la poudre de maquillage, le pharmakon inconsistant d'un corps pluriel qui ne tient plus à lui-même – ne pas rester auprès de soi, ne pas être à soi, voilà l'essence de la cendre, sa cendre même.

– Au-dessus du lieu sacré, l'encens encore, mais aucun monument, aucun Phénix, aucune érection qui tienne – ou tombe – , la cendre sans ascension, des cendres m'aiment, elles changent de sexe alors, elles s'andrent, elles s'androgynocident.

– Elle joue avec les mots comme on joue avec le feu, je la dénoncerais comme une pyromaniaque qui veut nous faire oublier qu'on construit des églises, en Sicile, avec la pierre de lave. L'écriture pyrotechnicienne feint de tout abandonner à ce qui part en fumée, ne laissant là que cendre à ne pas rester. Je placerais un long récit, des noms, Mallarmé, l'histoire du tabac, *La fausse monnaie* de Baudelaire, l'*Essai sur le don,* ''Toute l'âme résumée

– The fire: what one cannot extinguish in this trace among others that is a cinder. Memory or oblivion, as you wish, but of the fire, trait that still relates to the burning. No doubt the fire has withdrawn, the conflagration has been subdued, but if cinder there is, it is because the fire remains in retreat. By its retreat it still feigns having abandoned the terrain. It still camouflages, it disguises itself, beneath the multiplicity, the dust, the makeup powder, the insistent pharmakon of a plural body that no longer belongs to itself – not to remain nearby itself, not to belong to itself, there is the essence of the cinder, its cinder itself.

– Above the sacred place, incense again, but no monument, no Phoenix, no erection that stands – or falls –, the cinder without ascension, the cinders love me, they change sex, they re-cinder themselves, they androgynocide themselves.

– She plays with words as one plays with fire, I would denounce her as a pyromaniac who wants to make us forget that in Sicily churches are built with the stone of lava. Pyrotechnical writing feigns abandoning everything to what goes up in smoke, leaving there only cinder that does not remain. I would set out a long narrative, of names, Mallarmé, the history of tobacco, Baudelaire's "Counterfeit Money," Mauss's *The Gift,* "The whole soul summed up

de derrière ma voix, tu te rappelles, il y a tant d'années,
dans ma première 'vraie' lettre: 'brûle-tout.' ''

X

''. . . puis tu ajoutais) 'Je brûle. J'ai l'impression bête
de t'être fidèle. Je garde pourtant de tes phrases certains simulacres [depuis tu me les as montrés]. Je
m'éveille. Je me souviens des cendres. Quelle chance,
brûler, oui, oui . . .' ''

XI

''Le symbole? Un grand incendie holocaustique, un
brûle-tout enfin où nous jetterions, avec toute notre
mémoire, nos noms, les lettres, les photos, les petits
objets, les clés, les fétiches, etc.''

XII

''Holocauste des enfants.

                          Dieu lui-même
n'avait que le choix entre deux fours crématoires . . .''

XIII

''Ils n'y verront que du feu-.''

XIV

''Au bout du compte, première chance ou première
échéance, la grande brûlure de cet été. Tu seras là, dis-
moi, au dernier moment, une allumette chacun pour
commencer [. . .] Nous toucherons au feu un jour de

from behind my voice, you remember, so many years ago, in my
first 'true' letter: 'burn everything.' ''

X

''. . . then you added) 'I am burning. I have the stupid impression
of being faithful to you. I am nonetheless saving certain simula-
cra from your sentences [you have shown them to me since]. I am
waking up. I remember the cinders. What a chance, to burn, yes
yes . . .' ''

XI

''The symbol? a great holocaustic fire, a burn-everything into
which we would throw finally, along with our entire memory, our
names, the letters, photos, small objects, keys, fetishes, etc.''

XII

''Holocaust of the children

                          God himself
had only the choice between two crematory ovens . . .''

XIII

''They will only see it through the fire (they will only be blinded
by it).''

XIV

''In the final account, the first chance or the first reckoning, the
great burning of this summer. You'll be there, say it, at the last
moment, one match each to start. [. . .] We will draw close to the

63 . . .

grand pardon, peut-être, ce sera au moins la troisième fois que je joue avec ce feu jour-là, et chaque fois pour le départ le plus grave.''

XV

''Mais en principe seulement, et si la part du feu est impossible à délimiter, en raison du lexique et des 'thèmes,' ce n'est pas pour la raison habituelle (faire au feu sa part, allumer des contre-feux pour arrêter la progression d'un incendie, éviter l'holocauste). Au contraire, la nécessité du tout s'annonce . . .''

XVI

''. . . je n'y arriverai jamais, la contamination est partout et l'incendie nous ne l'allumerions jamais. La langue nous empoisonne le plus secret de nos secrets, on ne peut même plus brûler chez soi, en paix, tracer le cercle d'un foyer, il faut encore lui sacrifier son propre sacrifice.''

XVII

''et quand tu ne reviendras plus, après le feu, je t'enverrai encore cartes vierges et muettes, tu n'y reconnaîtras même plus nos souvenirs de voyage et nos lieux communs, mais tu sauras que je te suis fidèle.''

XVIII

''Ce fut sans doute le premier holocauste désiré (comme on dit un enfant désiré, une fille désirée).''

XIX

''Là où surtout je dis vrai ils ne verront que du feu. A propos, tu sais que la Sophie de Freud fut incinérée. Lui aussi.''

fire on a day of judgment, perhaps, it will be at least the third time that I play with the fire on that day, and each time for the most serious stakes."

XV

"But in principle only, and if fire's share is impossible to delimit, by virtue of the lexicon and the 'themes,' it is not for the usual reason (give fire its due, light counter-fires in order to stop the progression of a blaze, avoid a holocaust). On the contrary, the necessity of the whole [du tout] announces itself . . ."

XVI

". . . I will never get there, the contamination is everywhere and we would never light the fire. Language poisons for us the most secret of our secrets, one can no longer even burn at home, in peace, trace the circle of a hearth, one must even sacrifice one's own sacrifice to it."

XVII

"and when you will no longer come back, after the fire, I will still send you virgin and mute cards, you will no longer recognize even the memoirs of our travels and our common places, but you will know that I am faithful to you."

XVIII

"Doubtless this was the first desired holocaust (as one says a desired child, a desired girl)."

XIX

"There [Là] especially where I speak truly they will be blinded by the fire. On this subject, you know that Freud's Sophie was cremated. He too."

65...

XX

"Tomorrow I will write you again, in our foreign language. I won't remember a word of it and in September, without my having even seen it again, you will burn,

you will burn it,

it has to be you."

XX

"Demain je t'écrirai encore, dans notre langue étrangère. Je n'en retiendrai pas un mot et en septembre, sans que je l'aie même revue, tu brûleras,

tu la brûleras,

toi, faut que ce soit toi."

[. . .] pour peu Que la cendre se sépare [. . .] Le sens trop précis rature Ta vague littérature.''

– Par ces citations, ces références, vous autorisez la cendre, vous construisez une université nouvelle, peut-être. Écoutez plutôt Virginia Woolf, dans *Three Guineas:* ''L'argent gagné [par les femmes] ne devra en aucun cas aller à la reconstruction d'une université à l'ancienne, et comme il est certain qu'il ne pourra être consacré à la construction d'une université fondée sur de nouvelles bases, cette guinée portera la mention. 'Chiffons, essence, allumettes.' On y attachera cette note: 'Prenez cette guinée, et réduisez l'université en cendres. Brûlez les vieilles hypocrisies. Que la lumière du brasier effraie les rossignols! Qu'elle empourpre les saules! Que les filles des hommes éduqués fassent la ronde autour du feu! Qu'elles entretiennent la flamme en y jetant des brassées de feuilles mortes, et des plus hautes fenêtres que leurs mères se penchent et crient: Brûle! Brûle! Car nous en avons fini avec cette ''éducation''!' ''

– Encore faut-il savoir brûler. Il faut s'y entendre. Il y a aussi ce ''paradoxe'' de Nietzsche – qui en fait autre chose peut-être qu'un penseur de la totalité de l'étant – quand le rapport de la cendre au tout ne lui paraît plus

[...] however slightly The cinder separates itself [...] The overly precise meaning erases Your vague literature.''

– With these citations, these references, you authorize the cinder, you will construct a new university, perhaps. But listen to Virginia Woolf in *Three Guineas*: "No guinea of earned money [money earned by the women] should go to rebuilding the college on the old plan; just as certainly none could be spent upon building a college upon a new plan; therefore the guinea should be earmarked 'Rags. Petrol. Matches.' And this note should be attached to it. 'Take this guinea and with it burn the college to the ground. Set fire to the old hypocrisies. Let the light of the burning building scare the nightingales and incarnadine the willows. And let the daughters of educated men dance round the fire and heap armful upon armful of dead leaves upon the flames. And let their mothers lean from the upper windows and cry, Let it blaze! Let it blaze! For we have done with this "education"!' "

– One must still know how to "let it blaze." One must be good at it. There is also Nietzsche's paradox – which makes him something else perhaps than a thinker of the totality of entities *[l'étant]* – when he no longer normalizes the relation of the cinder to the whole by treating it as part of the whole, or by

régularisé par l'inclusion de la partie ou par quelque tranquillisant logos métonymique: "Notre monde tout entier est la *cendre* d'innombrables êtres *vivants;* et si peu de chose que soit le vivant par rapport à la totalité, il reste que, une fois déjà, tout a été converti en vie et continuera de l'être ainsi." Or ailleurs (*Gai Savoir*): "Gardons-nous de dire que la mort serait opposée à la vie. Le vivant n'est qu'un genre de ce qui est mort, et un genre très rare."

— Dans la première légende, qui vient à la seconde, après elle, le mouvement de la dédicace (reconnaissance de dette et non restitution) dit au moins, montre en disant à peine que la cendre vient à la place du don. Il y aurait eu don, même s'il n'est pas dit, comme il se doit pour qu'il ait lieu, de quoi ou de qui. Reconnaissance et dénégation d'une dette, d'"un seul trait divisé," "loin du centre." Et d'une lettre seule, d'un coup de dent en *d/t* ("Que la lettre soit forte en cette seule indirection") un centre s'effrite et s'attendrit, il se disperse d'un coup de dé: cendre.

— Muette, la dédicace feint de restituer. Mais elle ne saurait rendre ou donner rien que des poussières de feu, elle ne dit rien, elle ne laisse rien paraître d'elle-même,

introducing some tranquilizing metonymic logos: "Our entire world is the *cinder* of innumerable *living* beings; and what is living is so little in relation to the whole, it must be that, once already, *everything* was transformed into life and it will continue to be so." Or elsewhere (*Gay Science*): "Let us guard against saying that death is opposed to life. The living being is only a species of what is dead, and a very rare species."

— In the first legend, which comes after the second, after her, the movement of the dedication (recognition of debt and non-restitution) says at least, shows by barely saying that the cinder comes in place of the gift. Gift there would have been, even if it is not said, as it should be so that it may take place, from whatever or whomever. Recognition and denial of a debt, of a "single divided trait," "far from the center." And from a mere letter, indebted to a dental *d/t* flung from the tongue ("Though the letter gains strength solely from this indirection"), a center crumbles and melts, it is dispersed in a throw of the die: cinder.

— Mute, the dedication feigns restitution. But it only knows how to render or give nothing but fiery dust; it says nothing, it allows nothing of itself to appear,

de son origine ou de sa destination, qu'une piste de sable, et encore vous anesthésiant: sable brûlant ou pas? A la place d'autres, au pluriel déjà, de leurs noms et non d'eux-mêmes, il y a là cendre, "d'autres, il y a là cendre."

— C'est évidemment une figure, alors même qu'aucun visage ne s'y laisse regarder. Cendre de nom figure, et parce qu'il n'y a pas ici de cendre, pas ici (rien à toucher, aucune couleur, point de corps, des mots seulement), mais surtout parce que ces mots, qui à travers le nom sont censés ne pas nommer le mot mais la chose, les voilà qui nomment une chose à la place d'une autre, métonymie quand la cendre se sépare, une chose en figurant une autre dont il ne reste rien de figurable en elle.

— Mais comment un mot, impropre à seulement nommer la cendre à la place du souvenir d'autre chose, pourrait-il, cessant de renvoyer encore, se présenter lui-même, le mot, comme de la cendre, à elle pareil, comparable jusqu'à l'hallucination? Cendre, le mot, jamais ne se trouve ici, mais là.

— Il faut pour cela que tu le prennes dans ta bouche, quand l'émission du souffle, d'où qu'elle vienne au vocable, disparaît à la vue comme une semence brûlante,

of its origin or its destination, only a trail in the sand, and it still anesthetizes you: can you not feel the step [pas] into the burning sand? In the place of others, plural already, of their names and not of themselves, cinder there is, "of the others, cinder there is."

— It is obviously a figure, although no face lets itself be seen. The name "cinder" figures, and because there is no cinder here, not here (nothing to touch, no color, no body, only words), but above all because these words, which through the name are supposed to name not the word but the thing, they are what names one thing in the place of another, metonymy when the cinder is separated, one thing while figuring another from which nothing figurable remains.

— A word, unfit even to name the cinder in the place of the memory of something else, and no longer referring back to it, how can a word ever present itself? The word, like the cinder, similar to her, comparable to the point of hallucination. Cinder, the word, is never found here, but there.

— For that it is necessary that you take the word into your mouth, when you breathe, whence the cinder comes to the vocable, which disappears from sight,

une lave en vue de rien. Cendre n'est qu'un mot. Mais qu'est-ce qu'un mot pour se consumer jusqu'à son support (bande de voix ou de papier, autodestruction de l'émission impossible une fois l'ordre donné), jusqu'à se l'assimiler sans reste apparent? Et tu peux recevoir aussi la semence dans l'oreille.

— Quelle différence entre cendre et fumée: celle-ci apparemment se perd, et mieux, sans reste sensible, mais elle s'élève, elle prend de l'air, subtilise et sublime. La cendre – tombe, lasse, lâche, plus matérielle d'effriter son mot, elle est très divisible.

— Je comprends que la cendre n'est rien qui soit au monde, rien qui reste comme un étant. Elle est l'être, plutôt, qu'il y a – c'est un nom de l'être qu'il y a là mais qui, se donnant *(es gibt ashes),* n'est rien, reste au-delà de tout ce qui est *(konis epekeina tes ousias),* reste imprononçable pour rendre possible le dire alors qu'il n'est rien.

— Mon désir ne va qu'à la distance invisible, immédiatement "grillée" entre les langues, entre cendre, ashes, cinders, cinis, Asche, cendrier (toute une phrase), Aschenbecher, ashtray, etc., et cineres, et surtout la ce-

like burning semen, like lava destined nowhere. Cinder is only a word. But what is a word for consuming itself all the way to its support (the tape-recorded voice or strip of paper, self-destruction of the impossible emission once the order is given), to the point of assimilating it without apparent remainder? And you can also receive semen through the ear.

— What a difference between cinder and smoke: the latter apparently gets lost, and better still, without perceptible remainder, for it rises, it takes to the air, it is spirited away, sublimated. The cinder – falls, tires, lets go, more material since it fritters away its word; it is very divisible.

— I understand that the cinder is nothing that can be in the world, nothing that remains as an entity *[étant]*. It is the being *[l'être],* rather, that there is – this is a name of the being that there is there but which, giving itself *(es gibt ashes),* is nothing, remains beyond everything that is *(konis epekeina tes ousias),* remains unpronounceable in order to make saying possible although it is nothing.

— My desire only goes so far as the invisible distance, immediately "grilled" between languages, overrunning the distance between *cendre, cenere,* ashes, cinders, *cinis, Asche, cendrier* (a whole sentence), *Aschenbecher,* ashtray, etc., and *cineres* and above all

XXI

"Before my death I would give orders. If you aren't there, my body is to be pulled out of the lake [lac] and burned, my ashes are to be sent to you, the urn well protected ('fragile') but not registered, in order to tempt fate. This would be an envoi of/from me [un envoi de moi] which no longer would come from me (or an envoi sent by me, who would have ordered it, but no longer an envoi of me, as you like). And then you would enjoy mixing my cinders

XXI

"Avant ma mort je donnerais des ordres. Si tu n'es pas là, on retire mon corps du lac, on le brûle et on t'envoie mes cendres, urne bien protégée ("fragile") mais non recommandée, pour tenter la chance. Ce serait un envoi de moi qui ne viendrait plus de moi (ou un envoi venu de moi qui l'aurais ordonné mais plus un envoi de moi, comme tu préfères). Alors tu aimerais mêler

niza de Francisco de Quevedo, ses sonnets Al Vesubio, et ''Yo soy ceniza que sobró a la llama; / nada dejó por consumir el fuego / que en amoroso incendio se derama.'', se disperse, et ''será ceniza, mas tendrá sentido; / polvo serán, mas polvo enamorando.''

– J'entends bien, je l'entends, car j'ai encore de l'oreille pour la flamme si une cendre est silencieuse, comme s'il brûlait du papier à distance, avec une loupe, concentration de lumière à force de voir pour ne pas voir, écrivant dans la passion du non-savoir plutôt que du secret. Je dirais, pour la défense et illustration de sa propre phrase, moi la cendre, que le savoir n'intéresse pas son écriture. La cendre crue, voilà son goût; et la consonne initiale important peu, tout mot finissant par ( )endre, ou ( )andre, verbe, nom propre ou commun, et même un verbe quand il devient attribut – le tendre. Que fait-il avec DRE, je me le demande (sans, sens, sang, cent DRE). Je vous laisse chercher les exemples.

– Et avec ce lac, ces lacs, ce lacs – quand il y engage toute la télépathie, là aussi il y a LA Cendre.

– Non, vous traitez sa phrase comme l'accumulation d'une plus-value, comme s'il spéculait sur quelque

the *ceniza* of Francisco de Quevedo, his sonnets "To Vesuvius," and "I am cinder that darkens in the flame / nothing that remains to consume the fire / that in amorous conflagration is dispersed," that "will be cinder, but will remain sentient / will be dust, but amorous dust."

– I hear well, I hear it, for I still have an ear for the flame even if a cinder is silent, as if he burned paper at a distance, with a lens, a concentration of light as a result of seeing in order not to see, writing in the passion of non-knowledge rather than of the secret. I would say, for the protection and illustration of its own sentence, "I" the cinder would say that his writing is not interested in knowledge. The raw cinder, that is more to his taste; and the initial consonant matters very little; every word seems to finish with ( )inder, whether it's a common or proper noun, or even a verb, even a noun that we make into a verb – "tinder," "to tinder" – for the cinder makes every word "tinder." What does he do with DER? I wonder: (scin-, [pre]scin-, [re]scin-, DER). I leave it to you to find examples.

– And with this lack that is *la c*endre, these *lac*(k)*s*, this *lac*(k)(s) – when he gets all entangled with telepathy, there *[là]* also *LA C*inder is there.

– No, you treat his phrase like the accumulation of surplus-value, as if he speculated on some cinder

with what you eat (morning coffee, brioche, tea at 5 o'clock, etc.). After a certain dose, you would start to go numb, to fall in love with yourself, I would watch you slowly advance toward death, you would approach me within you with a serenity that we have no idea of, absolute reconciliation. And you would give orders . . . While waiting for you I'm going to sleep, you're always there, my sweet love."

mes cendres à ce que tu manges (café le matin, pain brioché, thé à 5 heures, etc.). Passé une certaine dose, tu commencerais à t'engourdir, à tomber amoureuse de toi, je te regarderais t'avancer doucement vers la mort, tu t'approcherais de moi en toi avec une sérénité dont nous n'avons pas idée, la réconciliation absolue. Et tu donnerais des ordres . . . En t'attendant je vais dormir, tu es toujours là, mon doux amour.''

Animadversiones I. *La dissémination* 408. II. *Glas* 265 sq. III. *La pharmacie de Platon*, in *La dissémination* 197. IV. *La pharmacie de Platon*, in *Tel Quel* 33, 59. V. *La carte postale* 271. VI. 7. VII. 9. VIII. 28. IX. 28. X. 28. XI. 46. XII. 155–56. XIII. 196. XIV. 213. XV. 238. XVI. 240–41. XVII. 262. XVIII. 271. XIX. 272. XX. 273. XXI. 211.

Animadversions I. Dissemination, trans. Barbara Johnson (Chicago: University of Chicago Press, 1981), 366. II. *Glas*, trans. John P. Leavey, Jr., and Richard Rand (Lincoln: University of Nebraska Press, 1986), 238–43. Translation modified. III. "Plato's Pharmacy," in *Dissemination*, 170–71. IV. "La Pharmacie de Platon," *Tel Quel* 33 (1968): 59. V. *The Postcard*, trans. Alan Bass (Chicago: University of Chicago Press, 1987), 254. VI. *The Postcard*, 3. Translation modified. VII. *The Postcard*, 5. VIII. *The Postcard*, 23. IX. *The Postcard*, 23. X. *The Postcard*, 23. Translation modified. XI. *The Postcard*, 40. XII. *The Postcard*, 143. XIII. *The Postcard*, 182. XIV. *The Postcard*, 198. Translation modified. XV. *The Postcard*, 222. Translation modified. XVI. *The Postcard*, 224. XVII. *The Postcard*, 245. XVIII. *The Postcard*, 254. XIX. *The Postcard*, 255. Translation modified. XX. *The Postcard*, 256. Translation modified. XXI. *The Postcard*, 196. Translation modified.

capital. It is, however, a question of making a withdrawal, in order to let him try his luck on a gift without the least memory of itself, in the final account, the remains of a body, a pile of cinders unconcerned about preserving its form, a retreat, a retracing only without any relation with what, now, through love, I just did and I am just about to tell you —

77 . . .

cendre capitale. Or c'est d'un retrait qu'il s'agit, pour laisser sa chance à un don sans la moindre mémoire de soi, au bout du compte, pas un corpus, un tas de cendre insoucieux de garder sa forme, un retrait seulement sans aucun rapport avec ce que maintenant par amour je viens de faire et je m'en vais vous dire —

77. We reprint the phrase "pas un corpus" from the 1982 text of *Feu la cendre* rather than "par un corpus" from the 1987 version. Both readings are, however, revealing in their own way. The gift on which one takes a chance is and is not a body; it is, rather, what remains of a corpse whose form is no longer decipherable. Was it ever?

These notes have been provided by the editor and are keyed to page numbers.

N o t e s

37. *Fors la cendre,* "nothing but the cinder," but also *for la cendre,* as in *le for intérieur,* one's innermost sense, thus "the innermost cinder"; *le four,* the furnace or oven, is not far off.

37. *Un lieu pur se chiffrât-t-il.* Derrida echoes the "taking place" of "place" (RIEN N'AURA EU LIEU QUE LE LIEU) *dans ces parages du vague,* "in these vague regions," from Mallarmé's "Un Coup de dés," where it is a question of hallucination, agony, and the unconcealment of the concealment of the origin of number (LE NOMBRE . . . *clos quand apparu*), where it is a question of "tallying up the whole" (SE CHIFFRAT-IL / *évidence de la somme*).

37. *Pur est le mot. Pur = Pyr,* Greek for "fire." Thus, *pyrification.*

39. *Tombe en tant que nom. Tombe,* as a noun, is "tomb"; as a verb, it means "falls."

41. *Encenser,* to praise or extol, as well as to burn incense, also sounds out *insensé,* insane or maddened; the English "incense" or "incensed" contains all these meanings.

53. "Clandestining" is the inevitable effect that the cinder *envoi* has on the sending of any letter.

55. "Rien du tout," "nothing at all," or "the nothing of the all."

57. Although the saying "il y a là cendre" appears in "Plato's Pharmacy" prior to its appearance in the dedicatory *envoi* at the very end of *Dissemination,* this allusion was in fact written after the one in the concluding acknowledgments. In distinguishing between the repetitions at work here, Derrida is reminded of Plato "mutter[ing] . . . [i]n the enclosed space of the pharmacy" as he begins to analyze the *pharmakon* [*Dissemination* 169]. In "Plato's Pharmacy" and more recently in "Chôra" [in *Poikilia: Études Offertes à Jean-Pierre Vernant* (Paris: Éditions de L'École des hautes études en sciences sociales, 1987), 265–96], Derrida presents *chôra* as

Plato's most challenging version of this "enclosed space," the "place" rather, the "mother and receptacle of this generated world" (*Timaeus* 51a), "there" between the unchanging Forms (*eidos*) on the outside and the mutable copies (*eikon*) on the inside.

59. "Cinders" makes the silent "s" in "cendres" audible. Here we might cite from T. E. Hulme's "Cinders," the final section of his *Speculations* (1924): "That the world is finite [. . .] and that it is yet an infinitude of cinders." Levinas has written of the Jewish custom of burying a faulty manuscript.

67. Derrida's caesura is formed from four of the fourteen lines of Mallarmé's sonnet, "Toute l'âme résumée," in *Hommages et Tombeaux,* where Mallarmé compares the expiration of the soul to the separation of the ash from the burning cinder (*la cendre se sépare / De son clair baiser de feu*) in a well-smoked cigar (*quelque cigare / Brûlant savamment*). Here lies perhaps a trace of the promised "history of tobacco." Incidentally, Baudelaire's prose poem, "Counterfeit Money," concerns a "singularly minute repartitioning" of the notion of the gift that occurs as two friends exit a tobacconist's shop. Derrida analyzes Mauss and Baudelaire in detail in *Donner le temps (Given Time)* (forthcoming).

69. The first Nietzsche citation is from notes made in 1881 during the composition of *The Gay Science* (Friedrich Nietzsche, *Idyllen aus Messina / Die fröhliche Wissenschaft / Nachgelassene Fragmente Frühjahr 1881 bis Sommer 1882,* in *Kritische Gesamtausgabe: Werke,* pt. 5, vol. 2, eds. Giorgio Colli and Mazzino Montinari [Berlin: Walter de Gruyter, 1973], 370–71).

69. The mortal throw of the die that is the exhalation of a vocable, at once delivers the gift and the debt, dissemination and grace, the necessity and impossibility of return; thus cinders fall to ash, "dé:cendre." The "thrownness" of Dasein is very much the work of the tongue.

71. "Sable brûlant ou pas," burning sand or not, also suggests the heat of the non-negative "step," the *pas,* the "stop" or obstruction to which we can be so anesthetized that we no longer feel the non-presence burning within language.

73. The "impossible emission" recalls, of course, the TV series *Mission Impossible.*

73. *Konis epekeina tes ousias* (cinders beyond being or presence) rewrites Plato's *agathon epekeina tes ousias* (The good beyond being).

73. "Griller une distance" means "to overrun a distance," here in the sense of being unable to stop because the very notion of a distance between languages has been annulled; the burning and the grilling begin as soon as one steps beyond *a* language and toward language itself.

75. "For the defense and illustration of the French language" is an expression of L'Académie Française.

75. "Tendre," like the English "tender" or "to tender," means something delicate or fragile that is extended or tendered within language; it rhymes with "cendre." Tinder and the neologism, "to tinder," make these motifs explicit and rhyme with "cinder."

75. *Sans* = without, *sens* = sense, *sang* = blood, and *cent* = one hundred, are all homonyms of *cen-dre*. "Scin-der" may suggest "scintilla," the slightest trace or spark, and the Latin "scindere," to cut or separate, and leads readily to "prescinding" (separation) and "rescinding" (annulment).

The English text *Animadversions* is set in Eric Gill's Joanna

types

The French texts **animadversiones** and **feu la cendre** are set in Max Meidinger's Helvetica

types

The English text **Cinders** is set in Matthew Carter's Galliard

types

Compositor: M. Meile

Designer: R. Eckersley

at the University of

Nebraska Press, 1991

50 years of publishing